DANTEWORLDS

12.60

Danteworlds

A READER'S GUIDE TO THE *INFERNO*

Guy P. Raffa

The University *of* Chicago Press :: Chicago & London

GUY P. RAFFA is associate professor of Italian
at the University of Texas at Austin and the author of
Divine Dialectic: Dante's Incarnational Poetry.

The University of Chicago Press, Chicago 60637
The University of Chicago Press, Ltd., London
© 2007 by The University of Chicago
All rights reserved. Published 2007
Printed in the United States of America

16 15 14 13 12 11 10 09 08 07   1 2 3 4 5

ISBN-13: 978-0-226-70267-4 (cloth)
ISBN-13: 978-0-226-70268-1 (paper)
ISBN-10: 0-226-70267-7 (cloth)
ISBN-10: 0-226-70268-5 (paper)

Library of Congress Cataloging-in-Publication Data

Raffa, Guy P.
    Danteworlds : a reader's guide to the Inferno /
Guy P. Raffa.
        p.   cm.
    Includes bibliographical references and index.
    ISBN-13: 978-0-226-70267-4 (cloth : alk. paper)
    ISBN-10: 0-226-70267-7 (cloth : alk. paper)
    ISBN-13: 978-0-226-70268-1 (pbk. : alk. paper)
    ISBN-10: 0-226-70268-5 (pbk. : alk. paper)
    1. Dante Alighieri, 1265–1321. Inferno. I. Title.
PQ4443.R24   2007
851′.1—dc22
                                        2006032999

Illustrations by Suloni Robertson.

♾ The paper used in this publication meets the minimum requirements of the
American National Standard for Information Sciences—Permanence of Paper for
Printed Library Materials, ANSI Z39.48-1992.

To my mother, Theresa Marino,
and in memory of my father, Gaetano Raffa,
and my grandparents:
Grazia, Giuseppe, Louise, and Placido

CONTENTS

Welcome to Danteworlds

WE ARE IN THE MIDST of a mini renaissance in the cultural appreciation of Dante's poetic masterpiece, the *Divine Comedy*. Hardly restricted to the rarefied air of higher education, this extraordinary interest in Dante Alighieri, an Italian poet from the late Middle Ages (1265–1321), is easily seen in the proliferation of new and recent works—translations, biographies, even popular novels featuring Dante or his poem—displayed on the shelves and Web sites of booksellers.

Naturally, this growing fascination with the man and his poem inspires many readers to learn more about Dante's world and the influences, events, and experiences out of which his vision of the afterlife was born. To gain a better understanding of the *Divine Comedy*, inquisitive readers (students and literature enthusiasts alike) most often rely on explanatory notes accompanying the poem or on the occasional book or essay written with a general audience in mind. The valuable notes provided with translations are generally limited (due to lack of space) to brief presentations of background information and concise explanations of difficult passages. Translations are sometimes accompanied by a separate volume of commentary, usually aimed at a scholarly audience, but these notes, like those placed after each canto of the poem or gathered together at the back of the book, still follow a strictly textual order, commenting on the poem canto by canto, line by line. Essays and book-length studies, while broader in scope and freer from a rigid textual chronology, are perhaps most useful to Dante's readers *after* they have already worked through the *Divine Comedy* at least once on their own or with a teacher and classmates.

Danteworlds takes a different approach. The project grew out of a desire to meet two basic challenges facing college students who read and discuss the *Divine Comedy*, in most cases for the first time, in the Dante course I teach one or more times each year: first, to become adequately familiar with the multitude of characters, creatures, events, and ideas—drawn from ancient to medieval sources—that figure prominently in the poem; second, to become adept at recalling *who* and *what* appear *where* by creating and retaining a mental map of Dante's postmortem worlds. My own experience, and that of my students, suggests that gaining such knowledge and skill while reading the *Divine Comedy* (especially the *Inferno*, with its many shades crowded into a finely divided space) serves as an indispensable foundation on which to build ever higher levels of understanding and interpretation. *Danteworlds* therefore provides entries on major figures and issues arranged so as to help you connect your textual journey through the poem with Dante's physical journey through the realms of the afterlife. This arrangement allows you to proceed geographically as well as textually, not only canto by canto but also—as Dante and his guides do—region by region through Hell, Purgatory, and Paradise.

Dante's readers have long recognized his powerful visual and encyclopedic imagination as a fundamental reason for the appeal of the *Divine Comedy*. Dante's poem, more than other depictions of the afterlife, takes us on a journey along with the protagonist by encouraging us to see and understand what Dante himself claims to have witnessed and learned as he descended through the circles of Hell, climbed the mountain of Purgatory, and visited the celestial spheres of Paradise. A letter from the late Middle Ages, addressed to the poet's most revered benefactor (Cangrande della Scala) during Dante's years of exile, offers general guidelines for reading and interpreting the *Divine Comedy*. Scholars disagree as to whether Dante or another well-educated person of the time wrote this Latin epistle, but few would dispute the letter's basic premise: in contrast to most (if not all) medieval accounts of otherworldly travel, the *Divine Comedy* famously insists on the literal, material truth of the protagonist's voyage as a basis for any other (allegorical) meaning. The more we know about the people and creatures Dante encounters, and the more precisely we envision the poet's representation of the afterlife, the better prepared we are to identify and understand additional meanings—sociopolitical, religious, philosophical, or personal—conveyed by and through the poem for posterity.

This book, created to enrich the experience of reading and discussing Dante's *Inferno*, the first part of his *Divine Comedy*, aims to assist readers of the poem in their interpretive journeys by providing an original, accessible commentary and study guide in a format uniquely suited to Dante's visual poetics. It is organized according to the geographic layout of Dante's representation of Hell: after the "dark wood" and a peripheral region just inside the gate of Hell, Dante's underworld is divided into nine concentric circles in the form of a large funnel (wider at the top), the last three of which are further divided into subcircles. The dark wood, the periphery of Hell, and the nine circles are each discussed in their own chapter, with one exception. Because circle eight, which Dante divides into ten subcircles (ditches or "pouches"), is so much more complex and crowded than other regions (over a third of the *Inferno* cantos are required to describe it), I thought it best to present the material for this circle in two chapters, the first covering pouches one through six, the second pouches seven through ten.

For each region of Dante's Hell, you will find a brief plot summary followed by entries explicating "encounters" and "allusions," significant verses (in Italian and English), and a series of study questions to aid comprehension and facilitate discussion of the poem. The "encounters" entries introduce the shades of dead men and women as well as assorted creatures (guardians, tormentors, symbols) whom Dante sees at this stage of his voyage, while the "allusions" entries cover other items essential for a fuller understanding and appreciation of the cantos under consideration: theological and philosophical ideas, historical and political events, classical and biblical references, and literary devices. For the reader's convenience, I include information about inhabitants of the region not seen by Dante but named by someone he does meet in the entry for the encountered speaker. The same holds true for future inhabitants of the region named by a spirit (yes, Dante's dead see into the future), with the exception of a few anticipated arrivals—such as Dante's archenemy, Pope Boniface VIII—who merit their own, more detailed entry in the "allusions" section.

In the *Danteworlds* entries, geographically arranged, you will therefore find valuable information on all the resident shades encountered by Dante (or named as current or future inhabitants) and on a host of other relevant topics. In preparing these entries, I consulted commentaries and studies by other Dante scholars in addition to the following standard reference works: Paget Toynbee's *A Dictionary of Proper Names and Notable Matters in the Works of Dante*, revised by Charles S. Singleton (Oxford: Clarendon Press, 1968), the monumental *Enciclopedia dantesca*, directed by Umberto Bosco (Rome: Istituto dell'Enciclopedia Italiana, 1970–78), *The Dante Encyclopedia*, edited by Richard Lansing

(New York: Garland, 2000), and *Medieval Italy: An Encyclopedia,* edited by Christopher Kleinhenz (New York: Routledge, 2004).

I based my decision on what to include in each entry first and foremost on a close reading of the encounter or allusion as it appears in the poem, and then on a careful examination of Dante's written sources, from the Bible and texts by classical authors to literary, philosophical, and theological works of the Middle Ages. I also made ample use of the earliest commentaries on the poem (produced within one hundred years of the poet's death in 1321), especially for news of people and events from Dante's time and place. For this, *Danteworlds* owes much to the online, searchable database of the Dartmouth Dante Project (http:// dante.dartmouth.edu), a magnificent resource conceived and directed by Professor Robert Hollander of Princeton University. I turned repeatedly to Dante's primary influences and first commentators to find and explicate material I believed most pertinent for enabling students and other readers to deepen their understanding of characters and allusions in the *Divine Comedy.* Hopefully, some of these entries will provide fresh insights into the poem and its relation to Dante's world and perhaps to our world as well. I tried to provide as much useful information as possible for each entry while still covering all the encounters and major allusions in the poem.

Ambitious readers will (and should) want more; to get you started, *Danteworlds* includes a bibliography of Dante-related materials: reference works, classical and medieval sources, Web sites, biographies and guides, and a selection of modern criticism and commentary with emphasis on the *Inferno* and Dante's cultural background. While most of these materials are written in English, a sampling of Italian works is provided for advanced students of the language.

In addition to following Dante's geographic representation of the afterlife, *Danteworlds* emulates the poem's own remarkable system of cross-referencing and self-commentary, the way in which figures and events that appear in later portions of the poem refer back (often explicitly) to previous episodes. Such internal recollections encourage readers to retrace their steps and observe the development of important themes. When a previously discussed character or allusion reappears within a later entry, the name or term, set in small capitals, is followed by a reference to the previous location. For example, the entry on Lucifer in the ninth and final circle of Hell includes cross-references to the GATE OF HELL (Periphery of Hell), JULIUS CAESAR (Circle 1, "Virtuous Pre- and Non-Christians"), and POPE NICHOLAS III (Circle 8, pouch 3). Note that for Julius Caesar the title of the earlier entry is provided ("Virtuous Pre- and Non-Christians"); the gate of Hell and Pope Nicholas III have separate entries under their names, but the mention of Caesar falls within a larger entry. To cite one such pattern of narrative echoes, the "Harrowing of Hell" (the story of Christ's descent into Hell to retrieve the shades of his biblical predecessors) is first told in Limbo (circle one) and then recalled, with new details, in circles five, seven, and eight.

The entries for each region of *Danteworlds* are followed by a selection of significant verses from the canto(s) describing the region and a series of study questions. The selected verses, many of which are among the most moving and meaningful lines of the *Divine Comedy*, appear in the original Italian followed by an English translation. Here is the famous opening line:

Nel mezzo del cammin di nostra vita (*Inf.* 1.1)
Midway along the road of our life

("*Inf.* 1.1" indicates canto 1, line 1 of the *Inferno*; this citation method is used throughout the book.) I attempt in my translations to respect the poet's renowned vernacular style and to assist the reader with little or no Italian by rendering Dante's original in modern, idiomatic English. The selected verses are intended to give readers (particularly those who are reading the poem in a translation with no facing-page original text) both a sample of Dante's own inimitable way with words and a place to begin to identify major ideas and themes. Thus the line just cited establishes the overarching journey motif of the *Divine Comedy*, underscores Dante's desire to relate his experience to his readers' lives ("*our* life" as opposed to "*my* life"), and raises the issue of a midlife crisis affecting the protagonist ("*Midway* along the road"). This last point is addressed in one of the study questions for the region (the "dark wood"). In fact, the selected verses frequently convey information useful for answering these questions.

The study questions are designed both to aid individual study and to foster group or class discussion. For example, most chapters include a question that asks you to explain the logical relationship between the sin of which the particular circle's inhabitants are guilty and the punishment to which they are subjected, a relationship (called the *contrapasso*) often suggested in one of the selected verses. Other study questions point to more challenging interpretive issues, such as Dante's own participation in a punished vice or the psychologically complex relationship between Dante and his guide, Virgil. In certain cases, a question explicitly asks you to reflect on similarities and differences between Dante's worldview and your own. For teachers and students, I hope some of these questions will lead to stimulating ideas for essay topics or research assignments.

Accompanying this book is a *Danteworlds* Web site (http://dante-worlds.laits.utexas.edu), created and hosted by Liberal Arts Instructional Technology Services at the University of Texas at Austin. The multimedia site contains, in addition to an abridged version of the entries in this book, Italian recordings of most of the selected verses and a vast gallery of images depicting characters and scenes from the entire *Divine Comedy*. Suloni Robertson, the artist who designed the map of Italy and illustration of Dante's Hell for this book, created many original images for the Web site (digital reproductions from her own paintings), the Inferno section in particular. Other images are drawn from works by Sandro Botticelli, John Flaxman, William Blake, and Gustave Doré, as well as from illustrations by an unidentified artist for Alessandro Vellutello's sixteenth-century commentary on the poem. Like this book, the *Danteworlds* Web site is structured around a geographic representation of Hell, Purgatory, and Paradise—the three worlds of Dante's *Divine Comedy*.

Having taught college classes on Dante's *Divine Comedy* for the past fifteen years, I find the geographic arrangement of entries in *Danteworlds*, combined with the study questions and selected verses, a highly effective way to help students prepare for class discussion, review for exams, and generate ideas for essays and research papers. Feedback from colleagues who use the *Danteworlds* Web site for their own classes has been similarly positive. I hope this guide and the accompanying Web site will contribute to the strong and growing appreciation of Dante's central place in world literature by serving as a valuable resource for readers of the poem at all levels of expertise.

I also hope *Danteworlds* succeeds in modeling and promoting the fruitful reciprocity of university teaching and research. To my delight, teaching the *Divine Comedy* to bright and demanding students while at the same time researching and writing *Danteworlds* has generated a two-way flow of knowledge between the classroom and my scholarship. There is just no substitute for revisiting the primary sources and historical events from the ancient world to the late Middle Ages that fired Dante's imagination and for examining closely how he refashioned this material into an enduring work of art. In short, I learned a great deal about Dante's poetry while producing the commentary for this book. I trust some of this learning will prove useful for my fellow Dante scholars as well as for students, teachers, and other impassioned readers of the *Divine Comedy*.

Major Events in Dante's Life

1265   Dante born under the sign of Gemini (late May–early June) in Florence

1270–75   Death of Dante's mother (Bella)

1274   First sight of Beatrice (who was born in 1266)

1281–83   Death of Alighiero, Dante's father

1283   Second recorded encounter with Beatrice

1285   Marriage to Gemma Donati, with whom he has three (perhaps four) children

1289   Present at the battle of Campaldino (as a horse soldier) and siege of Caprona

1290   *June:* death of Beatrice

1291–94   Studies in Florence with Dominicans (Santa Maria Novella) and Franciscans (Santa Croce)

1293–94   Writes the *Vita nuova*

1294   Meets Charles Martel, king of Hungary and heir to the Kingdom of Naples

1295–97   Enrolls in the guild of physicians and apothecaries. This allows him to enter Florentine political life, first as a member of the "Council of Thirty-Six" (which assists the *capitano del popolo*) and then as a member of the "Council of One Hundred" (charged with financial administration)

1300   Pope Boniface VIII proclaims Jubilee year.
       May: Florentine Guelphs splinter into "black" and "white" factions.
       June 15: Dante, a white Guelph, elected to the Council of Priors for a term of two months. (Easter week 1300 is the fictional date of the journey described in the *Divine Comedy*)

1301   *October:* travels to Rome as part of Florentine embassy to Boniface.
       November: detained as Charles of Valois (at Boniface's behest) enters Florence and allows black Guelphs to overthrow whites and sack the city

1302   *January 27:* sentenced to exile from Florence for two years and fined five thousand florins.
       March 10: permanently banned from Florentine territory under pain of death by fire

1303–7	In Verona, Arezzo, Treviso, the Lunigiana region (northwest of Lucca), and the Casentino region (north of Arezzo). *October 11, 1303:* Death of Pope Boniface VIII. *July 20, 1304:* Alliance of exiled white Guelphs and Ghibellines defeated at La Lastra outside Florence (Dante not present). Writes the *De vulgari eloquentia* and *Convivio* (both left incomplete)
1304–9	Conceives and composes the *Inferno*
1308–9	In Lucca(?), perhaps with his wife and children
1308–12	Conceives and composes the *Purgatorio*
1309	Pope Clement V moves the papacy from Rome to Avignon
1310–12	Henry VII of Luxemburg descends into Italy. Dante accompanies him on visits to several cities
1312–18	Resides in Verona in the household of Cangrande della Scala
1313	Death of Henry VII
1314	Publishes the *Inferno*. Implores Italian cardinals to return the papacy to Rome
1315	Refuses Florence's offer to allow him to return in exchange for admission of guilt and payment of a reduced fine. Publishes the *Purgatorio* and begins the *Paradiso*
1317	Writes the *Monarchia*
1318–21	In Ravenna as guest of Guido Novello da Polenta
1319–20	Exchanges Latin eclogues with Giovanni del Virgilio
1321	Completes the *Paradiso*. Contracts malaria during return from a diplomatic mission to Venice. Dies in Ravenna on September 13 or 14

Italy in the Thirteenth Century

Kingdom of Sicily
Papal States

Novara
Milan
Brescia
Treviso
Turin
Pavia
Verona
Venice
Mantua
Parma
Ferrara
Genoa
Modena
Bologna
Ravenna
Forlì
Lucca
Pistoia
Rimini
Pisa
Urbino
Florence
Ancona
Arezzo
Siena
Perugia
Assisi
Spoleto
Rome
SARDINIA
Benevento
Bari
Naples
Brindisi
Palermo
Messina
SICILY
Agrigento
Syracuse

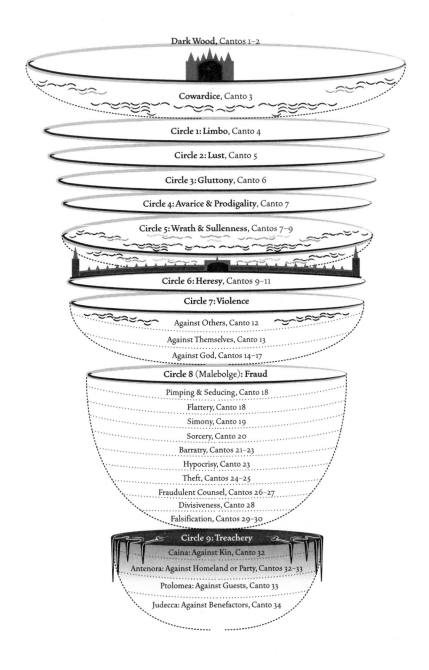

Dark Wood, Cantos 1–2

Cowardice, Canto 3

Circle 1: Limbo, Canto 4

Circle 2: Lust, Canto 5

Circle 3: Gluttony, Canto 6

Circle 4: Avarice & Prodigality, Canto 7

Circle 5: Wrath & Sullenness, Cantos 7–9

Circle 6: Heresy, Cantos 9–11

Circle 7: Violence

Against Others, Canto 12

Against Themselves, Canto 13

Against God, Cantos 14–17

Circle 8 (Malebolge): Fraud

Pimping & Seducing, Canto 18

Flattery, Canto 18

Simony, Canto 19

Sorcery, Canto 20

Barratry, Cantos 21–23

Hypocrisy, Canto 23

Theft, Cantos 24–25

Fraudulent Counsel, Cantos 26–27

Divisiveness, Canto 28

Falsification, Cantos 29–30

Circle 9: Treachery

Caina: Against Kin, Canto 32

Antenora: Against Homeland or Party, Cantos 32–33

Ptolomea: Against Guests, Canto 33

Judecca: Against Benefactors, Canto 34

IT IS EARLY SPRING in the year 1300 and Dante, "midway along the road of our life," has strayed off the straight path and finds himself in a dark wood. Heartened by the sight of a sunlit hill, he begins to climb to safety, but soon he is beset by a leopard, a lion, and a she-wolf and forced to retreat to the valley. Here Dante meets the shade of Virgil, the great Roman poet; to escape his dire predicament, Dante must visit the three realms of the afterlife, beginning with Hell, eternal abode of lost souls. Dante hesitates, declaring his unworthiness to undertake such a journey, but is persuaded to go when he learns that Virgil has been sent by Beatrice to rescue him.

Encounters

THREE BEASTS :: The uncertain symbolism of the three beasts—a **leopard** (or some other lithe, spotted animal), a **lion**, and a **she-wolf**—contributes to the shadowy atmosphere of the opening scene. Armed with information from later episodes, commentators often view the creatures as symbols, respectively, of the three major divisions of Dante's Hell: concupiscence (immoderate desires), violence, and fraud (though some equate the leopard with fraud and the she-wolf with concupiscence). Others associate the animals with envy, pride, and avarice. Perhaps they carry some political meaning as well (a she-wolf nursed the legendary founders of Rome—Romulus and Remus—and thus came to stand as a symbol of the city). Whatever his conception, Dante likely drew inspiration for the beasts from this biblical passage prophesying the destruction of those who refuse to repent their iniquities: "Wherefore a lion out of the wood hath slain them, a wolf in the evening hath spoiled them, a leopard watcheth for their cities: every one that shall go out thence shall be taken, because their transgressions are multiplied, their rebellions are strengthened" (Jeremiah 5:6).

It is perhaps best, at this early stage, to take note of the salient characteristics of the animals (the leopard's spotted hide, the lion's intimidating presence, the she-wolf's insatiable hunger) and see how they relate to subsequent events in Dante's journey through Hell.

VIRGIL :: As guide for his character-self through the first two realms of the afterlife (Hell and Purgatory), Dante chooses the classical poet he most admired. Virgil (70–19 BCE), who lived under Julius Caesar and then Augustus during Rome's transition from republic to empire, wrote in Latin and was (and still is) most famous for his *Aeneid*. This epic poem recounts the journey of Aeneas, son of a goddess (Venus) and a Trojan prince (Anchises), from Troy—following its destruction by the Greeks—eventually to Italy, where he founds the line of rulers that will lead to Caesar and the Roman Empire of Virgil's day. The poem, in fact, is in one sense a magnificent piece of political propaganda aimed at honoring the emperor Augustus. Two episodes from Virgil's epic were of particular interest to Dante. Book 4 tells the tragic tale of Aeneas and Dido, the queen of Carthage who kills herself when Aeneas abandons her to continue his journey and fulfill his destiny by founding a new civilization in Italy. Book 6, in which Aeneas visits Hades to meet the shade of his father and learn of future events in his journey and in the history of Rome, provides key elements of the spirit world, primarily mythological creatures and rivers, that Dante uses to shape his own version of the afterlife, Hell in particular.

Virgil also wrote four long poems, the *Georgics*, which deal mostly with agricultural themes (though they contain other important material, including the famous story of Orpheus and Eurydice in the fourth *Georgic*). And he wrote ten pastoral poems (the *Eclogues*), the fourth of which celebrates the birth of a wonderchild and was thus commonly interpreted in the Christian Middle Ages as a prophecy of the birth of Jesus.

Allusions

DARK WOOD :: Dante describes the dark forest (*selva oscura*) in which he finds himself at the beginning of the poem (*Inf.* 1.2) in vague terms, perhaps as an indication of the protagonist's own disorientation. The precise nature of this disorientation—spiritual, physical, psychological, moral, political—is itself difficult to determine at this point and thus underscores two very important ideas for reading this poem: we are encouraged, first, to identify with the character Dante and, second, to recognize that learning is a process in which we must sometimes read "backward" from later events to gain a fuller understanding of what happened earlier.

Characteristic of Dante's way of working, this "dark wood" is a product of the poet's imagination likely based on ideas from various traditions. These include the medieval Platonic image of chaotic matter, unformed and unnamed, as a type of primordial wood (in Latin, *silva*); the forest at the entrance to the classical underworld (Hades) as described by Virgil (*Aeneid* 6.179); the dangerous forests from which the wandering knights of medieval romances must extricate themselves; and Augustine's association of spiritual alienation with a "region of utter unlikeness" (*Confessions* 7.10) and temptation with "so vast a wilderness [*tam immensa silva*], so full of snares and dangers" (*Confessions* 10.35). In an earlier work (*Convivio* 4.24.12), Dante imagines the bewildering period of adolescence, in which one needs guidance to keep from losing the "good way," as a sort of "meandering forest" (*selva erronea*).

STRAIGHT WAY :: When Dante says he has lost the "straight way" (*diritta via*, also translated as "right way"; *Inf.* 1.3), he again leaves much to his reader's imagination. And again, in imagining the nature of this deviation, we may come to relate to the protagonist. In medieval thought, abandonment of the straight way often indicates alienation from God. Augustine, for example, views iniquity as a "perversion of the will" when it veers from God toward lower things (*Confessions* 7.16). However, in addition to any individual spiritual or psychological issues the phrase may suggest, the poet views such veering as a grand metaphor for the moral and societal woes of his world. Dante's notion of the straight way (and deviations from it) appears in all three realms of the afterlife as well as in the world of the living.

TIME OF THE JOURNEY :: Because Dante dates the initial action of the *Divine Comedy* to a point "midway along the road of our life" (*Inf.* 1.1), we know the journey took place toward the end of his thirty-fifth year: based on the biblical authority of Psalm 89:10 (Psalm 90 in the King James Bible), seventy years constitute a complete lifespan. Since Dante was born in 1265, his journey occurred in the year 1300, sometime not long before his thirty-fifth birthday (in late May–early June). Not coincidentally, Pope Boniface VIII proclaimed 1300 the first Jubilee, or Holy Year: pilgrims who, after receiving the sacrament of penance, traveled to Rome and (over a period of fifteen days) visited Saint Peter's and the basilica of Saint Paul outside the Walls were granted a onetime, full indulgence of all sins. Dante's entrance into Hell at the conventional midpoint of human life also echoes a biblical passage in which King Hezekiah, having been delivered from mortal illness, reflects on his tribulation: "I said: In the midst of my days I shall go to the gates of hell" (Isaiah 38:10). When Dante says he gained hope from the astronomical fact that the sun rose with the same stars that accompanied it at the moment of creation (*Inf.* 1.37–43), we can infer that the journey began under the sign of Aries, in late March or early April, the period in which the creation of the universe was traditionally believed to have occurred. (Information presented much later [*Inf.* 21.112–14] will allow us to pinpoint the time of the journey with even greater specificity.)

SIMILE :: Dante uses numerous similes (comparisons usually introduced with "as" and "so"), describing something that we are able to imagine to help us understand what he claims to have seen or felt. The first simile occurs in *Inferno* 1.22–27. Here Dante compares his narrow escape from danger to the experience of a man who, after arriving safely on shore, looks back at the sea that almost claimed his life.

SYNESTHESIA :: Meaning a "mixing of senses," synesthesia occurs when terms normally associated with one of the five senses are applied to a different sense. When Dante says he was driven back to the place "where the sun is silent" (*Inf.* 1.60), we wonder how the sun, usually associated with light and therefore sight, can have lost its voice.

GREYHOUND PROPHECY :: The greyhound (*veltro*) is the subject of the first of several enigmatic passages foretelling a savior figure who will come to restore the world to the path of truth and virtue (*Inf.* 1.100–111). Although Dante may be alluding to one of his political benefactors (Cangrande, whose name means "big dog"), he probably intends for the prophecy to remain as unspecific (and therefore tantalizingly open to interpretation) as the three beasts and the overall atmosphere of the opening scene. Virgil says the greyhound, feeding on "wisdom, love, and virtue," will destroy the ravenous and promiscuous she-wolf, thus preserving the Italy on whose behalf the following valiant warriors gave their lives: **Camilla**, queen of the Volsci, slew a number of Trojans in combat before being killed by Arruns (Virgil, *Aeneid* 7.803–17, 11.648–831). She fought alongside **Turnus**, king of the Rutulians, who waged war against the Trojans after Latinus, king of Latium, gave his daughter Lavinia (who had been promised in marriage to Turnus) to Aeneas; in the final scene of the *Aeneid*, Turnus is defeated by Aeneas in single combat and begs for his life, but Aeneas is reminded that Turnus killed a dear young friend (Pallas) and plunges his sword through the chest of his fallen foe (*Aeneid* 12.919–52). **Nisus** and **Euryalus** were Trojans celebrated for their devotion to one another. On a joint mission to bring a message to Aeneas, Euryalus was killed as the two men passed through the Rutulian camp; Nisus avenged the death of his younger friend before he too was killed by the enemy, his body falling on top of the corpse of his beloved comrade (*Aeneid* 9.176–445). All four soldiers therefore died in the Trojan-Italian war, recounted in the last six books of Virgil's *Aeneid*, two on the native Italian side (Camilla, Turnus) and two on the Trojan side (Nisus, Euryalus). By having the character Virgil alternate between affiliations (Camilla is named first, then Nisus, Turnus, and Euryalus), Dante implies that both sides in the conflict ultimately contributed to the greater good, the foundation of the future Roman Empire.

AENEAS AND PAUL :: Declaring himself unworthy to undertake this journey to the realms of the afterlife, Dante compares himself unfavorably to two men who were granted just such a privilege (*Inf.* 2.10–36). The apostle Paul claims in the Bible to have been "caught up into paradise" (specifically the "third heaven") where he "heard secret words which it is not granted to man to utter" (2 Corinthians 12:2–4), and Virgil describes the visit of AENEAS (see "Virgil" above) to the underworld in *Aeneid* 6. These two otherworldly travelers are linked through their association with Rome, seat of both the empire and the church.

Dante, contrary to Augustine and others, believed the Roman Empire in fact prepared the way for Christianity, with Rome as the divinely chosen home of the papacy.

THREE BLESSED WOMEN :: Similar to other epic poems, the *Divine Comedy* begins *in medias res* ("in the middle of events"). This means the events that prompted the journey happened prior to the opening action of the poem. In this case, Virgil explains in *Inferno* 2 that he was summoned to Dante's aid by Beatrice, who was herself summoned by Lucia at the request of a woman able to alter the judgment of Heaven (*Inf.* 2.94–108). This last woman, who sets in motion the entire rescue operation, can only be **Mary**, the virgin mother of Jesus according to Dante's faith. "Lucia" is Saint **Lucy** of Syracuse (died ca. 304), a Christian martyr closely associated with fortitude as well as sight and vision (her name means "light," and a later legend reports that she gouged out her eyes to protect her chastity). The common view that Lucy bore personal meaning for Dante (perhaps as his patron saint) derives from the poet's claim to have experienced a period of weakened eyesight as a result of intense reading (*Convivio* 3.9.14–16). **Beatrice**, who will reappear as a major figure later in the poem, was the inspiration for Dante's early love poetry and now plays the role of his spiritual guide. Early commentators have identified her as the daughter of Folco Portinari, an influential Florentine banker who founded the hospital of Santa Maria Novella and was chosen several times to serve on the commune's chief executive body, the priorate. Beatrice was married (in 1286 or 1287) to Simone de' Bardi, whose family ran one of Florence's largest banking houses. She died in 1290 at age twenty-four, just a year or so after the death of her father. Along with Virgil, these "three blessed women" (*Inf.* 2.124)—Mary, Lucia, Beatrice—make possible Dante's journey to the afterlife.

Significant Verses

Nel mezzo del cammin di nostra vita (*Inf.* 1.1)
Midway along the road of our life

Io non Enëa, io non Paulo sono (*Inf.* 2.32)
I am not Aeneas, I am not Paul

I' son Beatrice che ti faccio andare (*Inf.* 2.70)
I am Beatrice who makes you go

Study Questions

1 :: What do the three "Danteworlds"—Hell, Purgatory, Paradise—
mean to you? How do you envision them? How do you think they
might relate to one another and to the world in which we live?

2 :: Dante literally faces a midlife crisis. What problems or issues
do you associate with such an experience? Can you think of any
recent representations (in movies, books, the news) of some sort
of midlife crisis?

3 :: What might it mean that Dante describes himself as halfway
along the road of "*our* life," as opposed to "*my* life," in the opening verse of the poem?

4 :: Look for another example of synesthesia (soon after the first
one) in *Inferno* 1. What is the effect of these strange descriptions?
How do they contribute to the overall atmosphere of the opening
scene?

5 :: Discuss the similes in *Inferno* 1 and 2 (there are four in all). Explain how they work and why you find them effective or not.

Periphery of Hell: Cowardice

INFERNO 3

AFTER PASSING THROUGH the gate of Hell, marked with the ominous words "Leave behind all hope, you who enter," Dante and Virgil observe the many shades of those who lived such undistinguished lives they are refused entry to either Heaven or Hell. Racing after a banner that never comes to a stop, these cowardly souls are repeatedly stung by flies and wasps, their blood and tears becoming food for the worms at their feet. The travelers approach the shores of Acheron, where wretched souls of the damned gather to cross the river aboard a boat piloted by Charon. The quick-tempered ferryman denies passage to Dante, who, shaken by an earthquake, loses consciousness and collapses.

Encounters

COWARDS :: Included among the cowardly souls, who are also known as fence-sitters, wafflers, opportunists, or neutrals, are the angels who refused to choose between God and Lucifer (*Inf.* 3.34–42). The idea of a marginal place—inside the gate of Hell but before the river Acheron—for souls neither good enough for Heaven nor wicked enough for Hell proper is an original product of Dante's imagination. Partial theological justification for Dante's invention may be found in the Bible: "But because thou art lukewarm and neither cold nor hot, I will begin to vomit thee out of my mouth" (Apocalypse [Revelation] 3:16).

GREAT REFUSAL :: Observing the throng of cowardly fence-sitters, Dante singles out only the shade of one who made the "great refusal" (*Inf.* 3.60). In fact, he says it was the sight of this individual, unnamed yet evidently well known, that confirmed for him the nature of all the souls in this region. The most likely candidate for this figure is Pope Celestine V. His refusal to perform the duties required of the pope (he abdicated five months after his election in July 1294) allowed Benedetto Caetani to become Pope Boniface VIII, the man who proved to be Dante's most reviled theological, political, and personal enemy. An alternative candidate is Pontius Pilate, the Roman governor who refused to pass judgment on Jesus.

CHARON :: In the classical underworld (Hades), which Dante knew best from Virgil's *Aeneid,* Charon is the pilot of a vessel that transports shades of the dead, newly arrived from the world above, across the waters into the lower world. Like Virgil's Charon (*Aeneid* 6.298–304, 384–416), Dante's ferryman is an irascible old man—with white hair and fiery eyes—who at first objects to taking a living man (Aeneas, Dante) on his boat. In each case, the protagonist's guide (the Sybil for Aeneas, Virgil for Dante) provides the proper credentials for gaining passage: the Sybil presents the golden bough (*Aeneid* 6.405–7), and Virgil announces that Dante's journey is willed in Heaven (*Inf.* 3.94–96).

Allusions

GATE OF HELL :: It is not until the beginning of *Inferno* 3 that Dante finally enters the periphery of Hell (sometimes called the "Ante-Inferno" or "Vestibule of Hell") by passing through a gateway. The inscription above this gate—ending with the famous warning to "leave behind all hope" (*Inf.* 3.1–9)—establishes Dante's Hell as a creation not of evil and the devil but of his Christian God, here expressed in terms of the Trinity: Father (Divine Power), Son (Highest Wisdom), and Holy Spirit (Primal Love).

TERZA RIMA :: This is the rhyme scheme that Dante invents for the 14,233 lines of his poem. Literally translated as "third rhyme," this pattern requires that the middle line of a given tercet (a group of three lines) rhyme with the first and third lines of the next tercet. For example, in the verses of *Inferno* 3 describing the gate of Hell, *dolore* (line 2) rhymes with *fattore* (4) and *amore* (6), *podestate* (5) rhymes with *create* (7) and *intrate* (9), and so on. A single line, rhyming with the second line of the last tercet, ends each canto. *Terza rima* can thus be expressed by the following formula: *aba, bcb, cdc, ded . . . xyx, yzyz.*

ANAPHORA :: Dante occasionally repeats a word or phrase at the beginning of successive lines or tercets to drive home a point. *Inferno 3* opens with a striking example of this poetic device (called anaphora): Dante begins each of the first three lines, recounting the words written above the gate of Hell, with the phrase *Per me si va . . .* ("Through me one goes . . .").

ACHERON :: This is the first of the rivers and marshes of Virgil's underworld in the *Aeneid* that Dante includes in his topography of Hell. Whereas Virgil makes no clear distinction between the locations and functions of these bodies of water (Charon seems to guard them all), Dante's infernal rivers are more sharply drawn. Here the Acheron functions as a boundary separating the cowardly neutrals from the souls located below in the circles of Hell proper. Charon ferries these souls across the river. This attention to detail reflects Dante's desire to underscore the reality of Hell and his protagonist's journey through it.

Significant Verses

> Lasciate ogne speranza, voi ch'intrate (*Inf.* 3.9)
> *Leave behind all hope, you who enter*
>
> che visser sanza 'nfamia e sanza lodo (*Inf.* 3.36)
> *those who lived without shame and without honor*
>
> non ragioniam di lor, ma guarda e passa (*Inf.* 3.51)
> *let's not talk about them, just look and move on*

Study Questions

1 :: How does Dante's use of anaphora contribute to the overall tone and meaning of the inscription above the gate of Hell (*Inf.* 3.1–9) and to the reaction of Dante and Virgil to the ominous words (*Inf.* 3.10–21)?

2 :: What does Dante's invention of a region for cowards imply about Hell proper and its eternal inhabitants? What does this original idea say about Dante's view of human behavior and its relation to the afterlife?

3 :: Why do you think Dante refuses to name any of the shades, including the one who made the "great refusal" (*Inf.* 3.60), in this particular region?

4 :: How does the punishment of the souls fit their sin? Looking closely at *Inferno* 3.52–57 and 3.64–69, express the logical relationship between the sin and the punishment—what Dante will later call the *contrapasso* (*Inf.* 28.142)—in the form of a simile ("just as in life they…, so now in Hell they…") or in an ironic, causal phrase ("Because in life they failed/refused to…, now in Hell they…"). Try to imagine more than one interpretation for the *contrapasso* of the cowardly neutrals.

Circle 1: Limbo

INFERNO 4

AWAKING ON THE OTHER shore of Acheron, Dante follows Virgil into Limbo, the first circle of Hell. Limbo is set apart from the rest of Hell by its tranquil, pleasant atmosphere. It is the eternal abode of spirits from the pre-Christian world who led honorable lives, as well as of souls of unbaptized children and worthy non-Christian adults. Virgil is welcomed back to his home in a "noble castle" by a select group of classical poets, headed by Homer. After Dante himself joins this prestigious company, he views other famous figures from the ancient world (both historical and literary)—among them Plato, Aristotle, Pythagoras, Aeneas, Cicero, and Julius Caesar—and prominent medieval non-Christians, including a sultan of Egypt (Saladin).

Encounters

CLASSICAL POETS :: Among the magnanimous shades in Limbo is a distinguished group of four classical poets—**Homer** (flourished in the ninth or eighth century BCE), **Horace** (65–8 BCE), **Ovid** (43 BCE–17 CE), and **Lucan** (39–65 CE)—who welcome back their colleague Virgil and honor Dante as one of their own (*Inf.* 4.79–102). The leader of this group is Homer, author of epic poems treating the war between the Greeks and Trojans (*Iliad*) and Ulysses' adventurous return voyage (*Odyssey*). Although Dante had no direct familiarity with Homer's poetry (it wasn't translated and Dante didn't read Greek), he knew of Homer's unsurpassed achievement from references in works by Latin writers he admired. Dante knew works of the other three poets, who wrote in Latin, very well, particularly Ovid's *Metamorphoses* (mythological tales of transformations, often based on relations between gods and mortals) and Lucan's *Pharsalia* (treating the Roman civil war between Caesar and Pompey). Horace was best known as the author of satires and an influential poem about the making of poetry (*Ars poetica*). The vast majority of characters from and allusions to classical mythology in the *Divine Comedy* derive from the works of Virgil and of these writers, primarily Ovid and Lucan.

VIRTUOUS PRE- AND NON-CHRISTIANS :: In addition to the great classical poets, Dante witnesses a vast array of pre-Christian figures (and three eminent Muslims) whose notable achievements and virtues earn them eternal life within the quiet, verdant confines of a "noble castle." Dante and the five poets pass through seven gates in the seven concentric walls of the castle (perhaps symbolizing the seven liberal arts and the seven moral and intellectual virtues) before reaching a luminous, elevated position from which they can view the assembly of greathearted souls, divided into two broad groups, in the lush meadow below (*Inf.* 4.106–44).

The first group features men and women drawn primarily from Trojan-Roman military and political history, beginning with **Electra**, daughter of Atlas and mother of Dardanus, the legendary founder of Troy. Among Electra's Trojan descendants, Dante sees **Hector** (eldest son of King Priam), who led the Trojan forces against the invading Greeks until he was slain by Achilles, and AENEAS (Dark Wood), the hero of Virgil's poem who escaped Troy as it burned and journeyed to Italy, where he laid the foundation for the Roman Empire. During his visit to the underworld, Aeneas learned that his bloodline would eventually produce **Julius Caesar** (*Aeneid* 6.789–90), whom Dante considered to have become the first Roman emperor after he crossed the Rubicon, defeated Pompey, and consolidated power. CAMILLA was a virgin warrior-queen who fought valiantly against the Trojans on Italian soil (Dark Wood, "Greyhound Prophecy"), while **Penthesilea** was an Amazon queen who fought on the side of Troy against the Greeks in the earlier Trojan war (*Aeneid* 1.490–93). **King Latinus**, head of the native forces on the Italian peninsula that fought the Trojans, gave his daughter **Lavinia** in marriage to Aeneas, the victorious Trojan leader.

Lucius Junius **Brutus**, who avenged the rape of **Lucretia** (who subsequently committed suicide), the virtuous wife of Collatinus, by leading a revolt against the perpetrator (son of the Tarquin king) and his family line, became the first consul in the new Roman Republic. **Julia** (daughter of Julius Caesar and wife of Pompey), **Marcia** (second wife of Cato of Utica), and **Cornelia** (daughter of Scipio Africanus the Elder and mother of the tribunes Tiberius and Gaius Gracchus) were Roman women praised for their strength of character. Rounding out this first group, but isolated from these leading figures in Trojan-Roman history, is **Saladin** (Salah al-Din Yusuf ibn Ayyub), the distinguished Muslim military leader and Egyptian sultan who fought successfully against crusading armies in the Holy Land (capturing Jerusalem in 1187) and was admired even by his enemies for his chivalry and magnanimity. Dante praises Saladin for his liberality in *Convivio* 4.11.14, and Boccaccio features him positively in *Decameron* 1.3 and 10.9.

The second group, headed by **Aristotle** (see entry below), comprises shades of men known for outstanding intellectual achievement. Seated closest to the master in this "philosophic family" (*Inf.* 4.132) are **Socrates** and **Plato**, the latter of whom was Aristotle's teacher. Socrates (born ca. 470 BCE in Athens) was a legendary teacher known for the method of rigorous questioning that characterizes the dialogues of Plato (ca. 428–ca. 347 BCE), only one of which—*Timaeus*—was available (in an incomplete Latin translation) in the Middle Ages. Dante's knowledge of Plato, founder of the Academic School in Athens, was therefore based primarily on Latin commentaries and other works imbued with Platonic (and Neoplatonic) doctrine. **Democritus** (ca. 460–ca. 370 BCE), for whom the world was subject to chance (*Inf.* 4.136), believed the physical universe consisted of an infinite space filled with indivisible, eternal atoms functioning as a mechanical system based not on any intelligent design or purpose but on necessary laws. **Diogenes** (died ca. 320 BCE) was a leading member of the Cynics, a philosophical sect promoting virtuous living through self-control and the rejection of worldly comforts; when asked why he was carrying a lantern in broad daylight through the streets of Athens, he was reported to have said, "I am seeking an honest man." **Anaxagoras** (ca. 500–ca. 428 BCE), who believed the universe was formed by *nous* ("mind" or "reason") from the mixing of an infinite number of elements and the subsequent development of living beings, was also known for his cosmological theories, which included an explanation for the origin of the Milky Way (mentioned by Dante in *Convivio* 2.14.6). **Thales** (flourished sixth century BCE), a philosopher, statesman, mathematician, and astronomer renowned for seeking causes in the natural world (rather than in anthropomorphic gods), considered water the original and sustaining element of the created universe. **Empedocles** (ca. 490–430 BCE) believed that the four elements (fire, air, earth, water)—the building blocks of all matter—are separated by the force of strife and brought together by the force of love (with the created universe at a point of equilibrium between these two forces). **Heraclitus** (ca. 540–ca. 480 BCE), who emphasized the interrelations and balance of opposites (such as good and evil), considered fire the principal element uniting all things in the universe. **Zeno** most likely refers to Zeno of Citium (ca. 335–ca. 263 BCE), who founded the Stoic school of philosophy; Dante praised him as one of many philosophers devoted to wisdom (*Convivio* 3.14.8) but rejected his view that the ultimate goal of living is to pursue truth and justice with no display of emotions (*Convivio* 4.6.9 and 4.22.4).

Dante also sees the following shades in this gathering of eminent minds from Greek, Roman, and Islamic traditions (*Inf.* 4.139–44): **Dioscorides** (40–ca. 90 CE) was a Greek physician who gathered material for his major work, on the medicinal properties of plants, during his travels with armies of the Roman emperor Nero; this work was widely consulted in translation (*De materia medica*) in the Middle Ages and beyond. **Orpheus** was a mythical Greek poet and musician (from Thrace) whose song captivated the spirits and monsters of the underworld when he journeyed there to bring his wife Eurydice back to life (only to lose her again by looking back), a story well known to Dante from moving accounts by Virgil (*Georgics* 4.454–527) and Ovid (*Metamorphoses* 10.1–85); distraught over his loss, Orpheus withdrew from civilization, charming trees and rocks as well as wild creatures with his music, until—savagely killed by a horde of frenzied women enraged by his rejection of their love—he was able to reunite with his beloved in the afterlife (*Metamorphoses* 11.1–66). "**Tully**," short for Marcus Tullius Cicero (106–43 BCE), was a distinguished Roman orator, statesman, and philosopher; Dante frequently cites Cicero's treatises—particularly *On Friendship, On Duty, On Moral Ends,* and *On Old Age*—and the Roman writer provided a model both for the proper use of rhetoric (persuasive language) and for a literary representation of the celestial realm (in the "Dream of Scipio," the only part of Cicero's *On the Republic* available to the Middle Ages). Virgil pairs **Linus**, a mythical Greek poet-musician, with Orpheus in *Eclogue* 4.55–57 and praises him as a shepherd of "divine song" in *Eclogue* 6.67, while Augustine classifies both Linus and Orpheus as theological poets in *City of God* 18.14.37. Lucius Annaeus **Seneca** (ca. 4 BCE–65 CE), a powerful Roman statesman and prolific writer, was a tutor and advisor to the emperor Nero and the author of scientific and philosophical treatises promoting the Stoic life, as well as tragedies and moral epistles; Dante praises Seneca for his love of wisdom (*Convivio* 3.14.8), his demonstration of the dangers and inadequacies of wealth (*Convivio* 4.12.8), and his status as an illustrious teacher (*De vulgari eloquentia* 1.17.2).

Six figures round out this class of high intellectual achievers in Limbo: **Euclid** (flourished ca. 300 BCE) was a Greek mathematician whose *Elements* served as the authoritative source for geometric knowledge in Dante's day (in Latin, from Arabic translations of the Greek original) and for centuries thereafter; Dante not only cited Euclid on matters of geometry, such as the function of the point and the circle (*Convivio* 2.13.26), but praised the mathematician (together with Aristotle and Cicero) as one whose treatment of a topic was definitive (*Monarchia* 1.1.4). Claudius **Ptolemy** (ca. 100–ca. 170 CE), an Egyptian of Greek descent, enjoyed an equally authoritative reputation in the field of astronomy (Dante cites him in *Vita nuova* 29.2; *Convivio* 2.3.5–6, 2.13.25, 2.14.7); his *Almagest* presented a geocentric model of the universe (commonly known as the Ptolemaic system), which held sway until it was superseded by Copernicus's heliocentric model in the sixteenth century. Dante, following medieval tradition, considered the Greek physicians **Hippocrates** (ca. 460–ca. 377 BCE) and **Galen** (129–ca. 216 CE) the prime authorities on medicine (*Convivio* 1.8.5). The former was celebrated as the founder of Western medicine; the "Hippocratic oath," which sets out the physician's obligations, is ascribed to him, and his *Aphorisms* (short entries on diagnosis, prognosis, and treatment) were widely used in the Middle Ages. The latter, who at one time served the Roman emperor Marcus Aurelius, was renowned for making contributions, particularly in anatomy and physiology, that stood until the late

Renaissance. **Avicenna** (Ibn Sina; 980–1037 CE) and **Averroës** (Ibn Rushd; 1126–98 CE) were brilliant Muslim scholars. Avicenna was a precocious philosopher-physician of Persian descent (though he wrote mostly in Arabic), best known in the West for his *Canon of Medicine* and parts of his *Book of Healing*, though he authored nearly two hundred treatises on a wide range of topics; Dante cites him on, among other things, the generation of substances (*Convivio* 2.13.5) and the distinction between light and its reflected radiance (*Convivio* 3.14.5). Averroës, author of the "great commentary" on Aristotle (*Inf.* 4.144), was a Spanish Arab who, in opposition to the fundamentalists of his day, integrated Islamic and ancient Greek traditions to promote the philosophical study of religion; his argument for the immortality of the soul was deemed controversial (if not heretical) by Christian theologians who believed his concept of an eternal active intellect implies immortality of the human species but not the individual.

ARISTOTLE :: "The master of those who know" (*Inf.* 4.131): so respected and well known was Aristotle in the Middle Ages that this phrase is enough to identify him as the one upon whom the other prominent philosophers in Limbo, including Socrates and Plato, look with honor. Dante elsewhere follows medieval tradition by referring to Aristotle as "the Philosopher," with no need of additional information. Aristotle's authority in the Middle Ages owed to the fact that almost all his works were translated into Latin (from their original Greek or from Arabic) in the twelfth and thirteenth centuries. A student of Plato, tutor to Alexander the Great, and founder of his own philosophical school, Aristotle (384–322 BCE) wrote highly influential works on an astonishing range of subjects, from the physical universe, biology, and natural philosophy to politics, rhetoric, logic, metaphysics, and ethics. Next to the Bible, he was the most important authority for two of Dante's favorite Christian thinkers, Albert the Great and his student Thomas Aquinas, both of whom strove to validate the role of reason and to sharpen its relationship to faith. Aristotelian thought strongly influenced Dante in the content of a philosophical work (*Convivio*), the argumentation of a political treatise (*Monarchia*), and the moral structure of Hell (*Inferno*).

Allusions

LIMBO :: The concept of Limbo, a region on the edge of Hell (*limbus* means "hem" or "border") for those who are not saved even though they did not sin, existed in Christian theology prior to Dante, but the poet's version is more generous than most. Dante's Limbo (technically the first circle of Hell) includes virtuous non-Christian adults in addition to unbaptized infants. We thus find here many great heroes, thinkers, and creative minds of ancient Greece and Rome, as well as such medieval non-Christians as Saladin, sultan of Egypt in the late twelfth century, and the esteemed Islamic philosophers Avicenna (Ibn Sina) and Averroës (Ibn Rushd). For Dante, Limbo had also been home to major figures from the Hebrew Bible, who, as described in the following entry, were "liberated" by Jesus Christ following his crucifixion.

HARROWING OF HELL :: According to medieval Christian theology, Jesus Christ, following his crucifixion, descended into Limbo for the purpose of rescuing and bringing to Heaven his "ancestors" from the Hebrew Bible ("harrowing" implies a sort of violent abduction). Virgil supplies an eyewitness account, from his partially informed perspective, in *Inferno* 4.52–63. Among the many souls Virgil saw carried out of Limbo by Christ (whom Virgil identifies only as a powerful figure "crowned with a sign of victory"; *Inf.* 4.53–54) were Adam, Abel, Noah, Moses, Abraham, David, Isaac, and Jacob (Israel), along with Jacob's twelve sons and his wife Rachel. Since, according to Dante's reckoning, Christ's earthly life spanned thirty-four years, the Harrowing can be dated to 34 CE. Only suggested in the Bible, the story of Christ's postmortem journey to Hell appears in apocrypha (books related to but not included in the Bible) such as the Gospel of Nicodemus. So prominent was this story in the popular and theological imaginations that it was proclaimed church dogma in 1215 and 1274. Dante's version of the Harrowing, as we see from repeated allusions to the event during the protagonist's journey, emphasizes the power, in both physical and psychological terms, of Christ's raid on Hell.

Significant Verses

che sanza speme vivemo in disio (*Inf.* 4.42)
that without hope we live in desire

sí ch'io fui sesto tra cotanto senno (*Inf.* 4.102)
so that I was sixth among such intellect

vidi 'l maestro di color che sanno (*Inf.* 4.131)
I saw the master of those who know

Study Questions

1 :: Consider Virgil's behavior and his psychological/emotional state in Limbo. In particular, how do you think he was affected by the Harrowing of Hell (*Inf.* 4.52–63)?

2 :: What are the implications of Dante's self-identification as "sixth" among the great poets (*Inf.* 4.102)?

3 :: What does this region tell us about Dante's attitude toward the classical world and other religious traditions, such as Judaism and Islam?

Circle 2: Lust

INFERNO 5

DANTE AND VIRGIL encounter Minos, the monster who judges all the souls damned to Hell, at the entrance to the second circle. Tossed about by vicious winds, the spirits within this circle are guilty of lust, a sin that for many led to adultery and for at least some of the most famous—Dido, Cleopatra, Helen of Troy, Achilles, Paris, and Tristan—to a violent death. Here Dante is drawn to two lustful souls still bound to one another in Hell: the beautiful Francesca and her handsome brother-in-law Paolo were murdered by the betrayed husband. Dante is so distraught after hearing Francesca's moving tale of how she and Paolo came to act on their passion that he faints and falls hard to the ground.

Encounters

MINOS :: Typical of the monsters and guardians of Hell, Dante's Minos is an amalgam of figures from classical sources who is completed with several personal touches. His Minos may in fact be a combination of two figures of this name, one the grandfather of the other and both rulers of Crete. Admired for his wisdom and the laws of his kingdom, the older Minos, son of Zeus and Europa, was known as the "favorite of the gods." This reputation earned him the office, following his death, of supreme judge of the underworld. He was thus charged, as

Virgil attests, with verifying that the personal accounting of each soul who came before him corresponded with what was written in the urn containing all human destinies: "He shakes the urn and calls on the assembly of the silent, to learn the lives of men and their misdeeds" (*Aeneid* 6.432–33). The second Minos, grandson of the first, imposed a harsh penalty on the Athenians (who had killed his son Androgeos), demanding an annual tribute of fourteen youths (seven boys and seven girls), who were sacrificed to the Minotaur, the hybrid monster lurking in the labyrinth built by Daedalus.

Minos's long tail, which he wraps around his body a number of times equal to the soul's assigned level (circle) of Hell (*Inf.* 5.11–12), is Dante's invention. The original Italian of the first line describing Minos—"Stavvi Minòs orribilmente, e ringhia" (Minos stands there, horrifyingly, and growls) (*Inf.* 5.4)—is an arresting example of **onomatopoeia** (in which the sound of words imitates their meaning), as the repeated trilling of the *r*'s in "*orribilmente, e ringhia*" evokes the frightening sound of a growling beast.

FAMOUS LOVERS :: Physical beauty, romance, sex, and death—these are the pertinent elements in the stories of the lustful souls identified from among the "more than a thousand" such figures pointed out to Dante by Virgil (*Inf.* 5.52–69). **Semiramis** was a powerful Assyrian queen alleged (by the Christian historian Orosius) to have been so perverse that she made even incest a legal practice (*History* 1.4.7–8). She was said to have been killed by an illegitimate son. **Dido**, queen of Carthage and widow of Sychaeus, committed suicide after her lover Aeneas abandoned her to continue his mission to establish a new civilization in Italy (Virgil, *Aeneid* 4). **Cleopatra**, the beautiful queen of Egypt, took her own life to avoid capture by Octavian (the future emperor Augustus), who had defeated her lover, Mark Antony (she had previously been the lover of Julius Caesar). **Helen**, wife of Menalaus (king of Sparta) was said to have been the cause of the Trojan war: acclaimed as the most beautiful mortal woman, she was abducted by **Paris** and brought to Troy as his mistress. She betrayed the Trojans, including her new husband (Deiphobus married Helen after Paris was killed in the war), by helping the Greeks carry out their attack (Virgil, *Aeneid* 6.494–530). It is unlikely Dante knew the legend that a Greek war widow killed Helen (to avenge her husband's death); he may instead have believed she died during the sack of Troy. The "great **Achilles**" was the most formidable Greek hero in the war against the Trojans. He was killed by Paris, according to medieval accounts (Dante did not know Homer's version), after being tricked into entering the temple of Apollo to meet the Trojan princess Polyxena. **Tristan**, nephew of King Mark of Cornwall, and Iseult (Mark's fiancée) became lovers after they mistakenly drank the magic potion intended for Mark and Iseult. Mark shot Tristan with a poisoned arrow, according to one version of the story popular in Dante's day, and the wounded man then clenched his lover so tightly that they died in one another's arms.

FRANCESCA AND PAOLO :: Francesca da Rimini and Paolo Malatesta are punished together in the second circle for their adultery. But, Francesca's shade tells Dante, her husband—Paolo's brother Gianciotto ("Crippled John")—is destined for punishment in Caina, a lower infernal realm named after Cain, who killed his brother Abel (Genesis 4:8). Francesca was the aunt of Guido Novello da Polenta, Dante's host in Ravenna during the last years of the poet's life (1318–21). She was married (ca. 1275) for political reasons to Gianciotto of the powerful Malatesta family, rulers of Rimini. Dante may have actually met Paolo in Florence in 1282 (when Paolo was *capitano del popolo*, a political office assigned to citizens of other cities), not long before he and Francesca were killed by Gianciotto.

Although no version of Francesca's story is known to have existed before Dante, Giovanni Boccaccio, a generation or two after Dante, provides a "historical" account of the events behind Francesca's presentation that would not be out place among the sensational novellas of his prose masterpiece, the *Decameron*. Even if there is more fiction than fact in Boccaccio's account, it helps explain the character Dante's emotional response to Francesca's story by presenting her in a sympathetic light. Francesca, according to Boccaccio, was blatantly tricked into marrying Gianciotto, who was disfigured and uncouth, when the handsome and elegant Paolo was sent in his brother's place to settle the nuptial contract. Angered at finding herself wed the following day to Gianciotto, Francesca made no attempt to restrain her affections for Paolo and the two in fact soon became lovers. Informed of this liaison, Gianciotto one day caught his brother and Francesca together in her bedroom when she, unaware that Paolo had become stuck as he tried to escape through a trapdoor, let her husband enter the room. Gianciotto lunged at Paolo with a sword, but Francesca stepped between the two men and was killed instead, much to the dismay of her husband, who then promptly finished off Paolo. Francesca and Paolo, Boccaccio concludes, were buried—accompanied by many tears—in a single tomb. Francesca's eloquent description of the power of love (*Inf.* 5.100–107), emphasized through the use of ANAPHORA (Periphery of Hell), bears much the same meaning and style as the love poetry once admired by Dante and of which he himself produced many fine examples.

Allusions

LUST :: Here Dante explores the relationship, as notoriously challenging in his time and place as in ours, between love and lust, between the ennobling power of attraction toward the beauty of a whole person and the destructive force of possessive sexual desire. The lustful in Hell, whose actions often led them and their lovers to death, are "carnal sinners who subordinate reason to desire" (*Inf.* 5.38–39). From the examples presented, it appears that for Dante a line is crossed when one *acts* on this desire. The poet, more convincingly than most moralists and theologians, shows that this line is a very fine one indeed, and he acknowledges the potential complicity (his own included) of those who promulgate ideas and images of romantic love through their creative work. Dante's placement of lust, one of the seven capital sins (sometimes called "mortal" or "deadly" sins), in the first circle of Hell in which an unrepented sin is punished (the second circle overall) is similarly ambiguous: on the one hand, lust is the sin farthest from Satan, which marks it as the least serious sin in Hell (and in life); on the other hand, it is the first sin presented, which recalls the common, if crude, association of sex with original sin, that is, with the fall of humankind (Adam and Eve) in the Garden of Eden.

LANCELOT AND GUINEVERE :: The story of Lancelot and Guinevere, which Francesca identifies as the catalyst for her affair with

Paolo (*Inf.* 5.127–38), was a French romance popular both in poetry (by Chrétien de Troyes) and in a prose version known as *Lancelot of the Lake*. According to this prose text, it is Queen Guinevere, wife of King Arthur, who kisses Lancelot, the most valiant of Arthur's Knights of the Round Table. Francesca, by giving the romantic initiative to Paolo, reverses the roles. To her mind, the book recounting this famous love affair performs a function similar to that of the character **Gallehaut**, a friend of Lancelot who helps bring about the adulterous relationship between the queen and her husband's favorite knight.

Significant Verses

Stavvi Minòs orribilmente, e ringhia (*Inf.* 5.4)
Minos stands there, horrifyingly, and growls

Galeotto fu 'l libro e chi lo scrisse:
quel giorno piú non vi leggemmo avante (*Inf.* 5.137–38)
*a Gallehaut was the book and he who wrote it:
that day we read no more of it*

E caddi come corpo morto cade (*Inf.* 5.142)
And I fell the way a dead body falls

Study Questions

1 :: Following their judgment by Minos, how do you imagine the souls travel to their destined location in Hell for eternal punishment? Might Minos's tail be somehow involved in this unexplained event?

2 :: What is the *contrapasso* for circle two of Dante's Hell, the logical relationship between the vice of lust and its punishment?

3 :: Why is Dante moved to tears after Francesca's description of love (*Inf.* 5.109–17)? Why does he fall "the way a dead body falls" after her personal account of an intimate relationship with Paolo (*Inf.* 5.139–42)?

4 :: The episode of Francesca and Paolo, the first in which Dante encounters someone punished in Hell for their sins, presents a challenge: Dante the character is overcome by compassion for the lovers even as Dante the poet has damned them to Hell in the first place. What are possible consequences of this apparent gap between the perspectives of the character and the poet who are both "Dante"?

5 :: Dante's presentation of Francesca and Paolo encourages us to consider the place of moral responsibility in depictions of love, sex, and violence in our own day. We can certainly discuss music, television, movies, and advertising (as well as literature) in these terms. Who is more (or less) responsible and therefore accountable for unacceptable attitudes and behavior in society: the creators and vehicles of such messages or their consumers and audiences?

Circle 3: Gluttony

INFERNO 6

CERBERUS, A DOGLIKE BEAST with three heads, guards the third circle of Hell and mauls the spirits punished here for their gluttony. The shades, writhing in muck, are unrelentingly pounded by a cold and filthy mixture of rain, sleet, and snow that makes the earth stink. One glutton, nicknamed Ciacco, rises up and recognizes Dante as a fellow Florentine. Ciacco prophesies bloody fighting between Florence's two political factions that will result first in the supremacy of one party (white Guelphs) and then, less than three years later, the victory and harsh retribution of the other party (black Guelphs). After informing Dante that several leading Florentines are punished below in other circles of Hell, Ciacco falls back to the ground, not to rise again until the Last Judgment at the end of time.

Encounters

CERBERUS :: In the *Aeneid* Virgil describes Cerberus, a three-headed dog who guards the entrance to the classical underworld, as loud, huge, and terrifying (with snakes rising from his neck). To get by Cerberus, the Sybil (Aeneas's guide) feeds him a spiked honey-cake that makes him immediately fall asleep (*Aeneid* 6.417–25). Dante's Cerberus, who mangles the shades in the circle of gluttony, also displays canine qualities: his three throats produce a deafening bark, and he eagerly devours—like a dog intent on his meal—the fistfuls of dirt that Virgil throws into his mouths. Other aspects of Cerberus's appearance, such as his red eyes (bloodshot?), greasy black beard, large gut, and clawed hands (*Inf.* 6.16–17), perhaps link him to the gluttonous spirits who suffer in the sixth circle.

CIACCO :: The name Ciacco, apparently a nickname for the poet's gluttonous acquaintance, could be a shortened form of Giacomo or perhaps a derogatory reference, meaning "hog" or "pig" in the Florentine dialect of Dante's day. Dante, who exploits the common medieval belief in the essential relationship between names and the things (or people) they represent, at times chooses characters for particular locations in the afterlife based at least in part on their names. "Ciacco" may be the first case of this sort in the poem. Apart from what Dante writes in *Inferno* 6, we know very little of Ciacco's life. Boccaccio claims that, despite his gluttony (for which he was notorious), Ciacco was respected in polite Florentine society for his eloquence and agreeableness. Another early commentator (Benvenuto) remarks that the Florentines were known for their traditionally temperate attitude toward food and drink, but that when they fell, they fell hard and surpassed all others in their gluttony. Dante learns from Ciacco that a number of prominent Florentines, including Farinata, Tegghiaio, Rusticucci, Arrigo, and Mosca, are "among the blackest souls" in Hell despite their desire to do good (*Inf.* 6.79–87). Dante will encounter four of these five worthy men (he will not see Arrigo) in lower circles of Hell.

Allusions

GLUTTONY :: Gluttony, like lust, is one of the seven capital sins according to medieval Christian theology and church practice. Dante, at least in circles two through five of Hell, uses these sins as part (but only part) of his organizational strategy. Although lust and gluttony were generally considered the least serious of the seven sins (and pride almost always the worst), their order was not consistent: some writers thought lust was worse than gluttony, while others thought gluttony worse than lust. Based on the biblical precedent of Eve "eating" the forbidden fruit and then successfully "tempting" Adam to do so (Genesis 3:6), gluttony and lust were often viewed as closely related to one another. Gluttony is usually understood as referring to excessive eating and drinking; from the less than obvious *contrapasso* for the gluttons and the content (mostly political) of *Inferno* 6, Dante appears to view it as something more complex.

FLORENTINE POLITICS (1300–1302) :: Spring of 1300 is the approximate fictional date of the journey (see Dark Wood, "Time of the Journey"). At that time Florence was politically divided between two rival factions known as white and black Guelphs. The conflict originated in a feud between two leading Florentine families and their followers, the black faction led by the aristocrat Corso Donati, the white faction by the banker Vieri dei Cerchi. Although class and social distinctions between the two groups quickly diminished in importance (there were rich merchants who supported Donati and noblemen who supported Cerchi), ideological differences proved to be irreconcilable: black Guelphs benefited economically and politically from strengthening traditional alliances with the papacy and the French house of Anjou, while white Guelphs firmly resisted papal and Angevin ambitions and favored better relations with Ghibelline cities. Ciacco (*Inf.* 6.64–72) provides the first of several important prophecies in the poem of the struggle between these two groups that will result in Dante's permanent exile from Florence (from 1302 until his death in 1321). The white Guelphs—the "party of the woods" because of the rural origins of the Cerchi, their leading clan—were in charge in May 1300, when skirmishes broke out between the two factions. Although ringleaders from both parties were punished by banishment (Dante, a white Guelph, was part of the city government that made this decision), by spring of the following year (1301) most of the white Guelphs had returned, while leading black Guelphs were forced to remain in exile. However, the tables were soon turned; by 1302 ("within three suns" from the riots of 1300) six hundred leading white Guelphs (Dante among them) were forced into exile. The black Guelphs prevailed because they were supported by Charles of Valois, a French prince sent by Pope Boniface

VIII ostensibly to bring peace to Florence but actually to instigate the violent overthrow of the white Guelph leadership.

LAST JUDGMENT :: When Virgil tells Dante that Ciacco will not rise again until the "sound of the angelic trumpet" and the arrival of the "enemy ruler" (*Inf.* 6.94–96), he is alluding to the Last Judgment. Also called the Apocalypse and the Second Coming of Christ, the Last Judgment in the medieval Christian imagination marks the end of time, when God comes (as Christ) to judge all human souls and separate the saved from the damned. Scripturally based on Matthew 25:31–46 and the Apocalypse (Revelation), this event is frequently depicted in art and literature of the Middle Ages and Renaissance, most famously in Michelangelo's frescoed wall in the Sistine Chapel in Rome. The young Dante would have had ample opportunity to reflect on the Last Judgment from his observation of its terrifying representation on the ceiling of the Florentine baptistery. According to the accepted theology of Dante's day, souls would be judged immediately after death and would then proceed either to Hell (if damned) or Purgatory (if saved); this judgment would be confirmed at the end of time, and all souls would then spend eternity either in Hell or in Heaven (as Purgatory would cease to exist). The *Divine Comedy* presents the state of souls sometime between these two judgments. In *Inferno* 6 we learn, along with the character Dante, that the souls of the dead will be reunited with their bodies at the end of time. The suffering of the damned, and the joy of the blessed, will then increase because the individual is complete and therefore more perfect (*Inf.* 6.103–11).

Significant Verses

Voi cittadini mi chiamaste Ciacco (*Inf.* 6.52)
You Florentines called me Ciacco

piú non ti dico e piú non ti rispondo (*Inf.* 6.90)
I tell you no more and I no longer answer you

Study Questions

1 :: How has Dante transformed Cerberus to fit the role of guardian in the circle of gluttony (*Inf.* 6.13–33)? How does this figure shed light on Dante's conception of the sin?

2 :: Describe the *contrapasso* (the relationship between the vice and its punishment) for gluttony.

3 :: Look at lines 55–57, 76–78, and 90 of *Inferno* 6. How might Dante figuratively participate in the sin by displaying gluttonous behavior himself?

Circle 4: Avarice & Prodigality

INFERNO 7

PLUTUS, A WOLFLIKE BEAST, shouts a warning to Satan as Dante and Virgil enter the fourth circle of Hell, but Virgil's harsh rebuke silences him and allows the travelers to pass unscathed. Dante now sees a multitude of shades damned for the sin of avarice (holding wealth too tightly) or its opposite, prodigality (spending too freely). The two groups push heavy boulders with their chests around a circle in opposite directions: when the avaricious and the prodigal collide, they turn and, after casting insults at one another, repeat the journey in the other direction. So filthy have the souls become as a result of their sordid lives that Dante cannot recognize them individually, though Virgil reports the presence of many clerics, including cardinals and popes, among the avaricious. He also explains to Dante the divine role of Fortuna in human affairs.

Encounter

PLUTUS :: Dante's Plutus, guardian-symbol of the fourth circle, is, like other infernal creatures, a unique hybrid of sources and natures. Often portrayed as the mythological god of the classical underworld (Hades),

Plutus also appears in some cases as the god of wealth. Dante neatly merges these two figures by making Plutus the "great enemy" (*Inf.* 6.115), with a special relationship to the sin most closely associated with material wealth. Dante similarly combines human and bestial natures in his depiction (*Inf.* 7.1–15): Plutus possesses the power of speech (though the precise meaning of his words—some sort of invocation to Satan—is unclear) and the ability to understand (or at least react to) Virgil's dismissive words, while at the same time displaying animal features and a distinctly bestial rage.

Allusions

AVARICE AND PRODIGALITY :: Avarice, or greed (lust for material gain), is one of the iniquities that most incurs Dante's scorn and wrath. Consistent with the biblical saying that avarice is "the root of all evils" (1 Timothy 6:10), medieval Christian thought viewed the sin as most offensive to the spirit of love; Dante goes even further by blaming avarice for the ethical and political corruption in his society. Ciacco identifies avarice, along with pride and envy, as one of the primary vices enflaming Florentine hearts (*Inf.* 6.74–75), and the poet consistently condemns greed and its effects throughout the *Divine Comedy*. Whereas his condemnation of lust and gluttony was tempered by sympathy for FRANCESCA (Circle 2) and CIACCO (Circle 3), Dante shows no mercy in selecting avarice as the capital sin punished in the fourth circle of Hell. He pointedly presents the sin as a common vice of monks and church leaders (including cardinals and popes), and he further degrades the sinners by making them so physically squalid that they are unrecognizable to the travelers (*Inf.* 7.49–54). By defining the sin as "spending without measure" (*Inf.* 7.42), Dante for the first time applies the classical principle of moderation (or the "golden mean") to criticize excessive desire for neutral objects, as manifested both in "closed fists" (avarice) and in spending too freely (prodigality). Fittingly, these two groups punish and insult one another in the afterlife.

FORTUNA :: Consistent with his devastating indictment of sinful attitudes toward material wealth, Dante has a very strong and original idea of the role of fortune in human affairs (*Inf.* 7.61–96). Fortune is certainly a powerful force in earlier philosophy and literature, most notably in Boethius's *Consolation of Philosophy*. Dante claims to have read this Latin work, which was highly influential throughout the Middle Ages, in the difficult period following the death of his beloved BEATRICE (Dark Wood, "Three Blessed Women"). Boethius presents Fortuna as a fickle and mischievous goddess who delights in her ability to change an individual's circumstances (for good or ill) on a whim. It is far more constructive, according to Boethius (who has been unjustly deprived of his possessions, honors, and freedom), to ignore one's earthly status altogether and trust only in what is certain and immutable. Adverse fortune is ultimately better than good fortune because it is more effective in teaching this lesson.

Dante's Fortuna is also female, but he imagines her as an angelic intelligence (a "divine minister") who guides the distribution of worldly goods, just as God's light and goodness are distributed throughout the created universe. She is above the fray, immune to both praise and blame from those who experience the ups and downs that result from her actions. Much as Dante "demonizes" many mythological creatures from the classical underworld, he "deifies" the traditional representation of fortune. The ways of fortune, like the application of divine justice generally, are simply beyond the capacity of human understanding.

Significant Verses

gridando: "Perché tieni?" e "Perché burli?" (*Inf.* 7.30)
[*They were*] *crying out: "Why hoard?" and "Why waste?"*

volve sua spera e beata si gode (*Inf.* 7.96)
she turns her sphere and rejoices in her blessedness

Study Questions

1 :: Draw an image of the punishment of the avaricious and the prodigal as described in *Inferno* 7.22–35.

2 :: Taking into account Virgil's description of fortune in *Inferno* 7.73–96, explain how this punishment is appropriate for the vices of circle four.

Circle 5: Wrath & Sullenness

INFERNO 7–9

DANTE SEES WRATHFUL SOULS battering and biting one another in the swampy waters of the Styx, the fifth circle of Hell, and he learns that the bubbles on the surface are caused by sullen spirits stuck in the muddy bottom of the marsh. The travelers cross the Styx in a swift vessel piloted by Phlegyas. When Filippo Argenti, an arrogant Florentine whom Dante knows and detests, rises up and threatens to grab the boat, Virgil shoves him back into the water where he is soon slaughtered by his wrathful cohorts, much to Dante's delight. The resentful boatman deposits Dante and Virgil at the entrance to Dis, the fortressed city of Lower Hell. Over a thousand fallen angels who guard the entrance refuse entry to the travelers, slamming the gate in Virgil's face. Bloodcurdling Furies then appear above the walls and call on Medusa to come and turn Dante to stone. However, a messenger from Heaven arrives to squelch the resistance and open the gate, thus allowing Dante and Virgil to visit the circles of Lower Hell.

Encounters

PHLEGYAS (8) :: The infernal employee who transports Dante and Virgil in his boat across the Styx (*Inf.* 8.13–24), circle of the wrathful and sullen, is appropriately known for his own impetuous (if understandable) behavior. In a fit of rage, Phlegyas set fire to the temple of Apollo because the god had raped his daughter. Apollo promptly slew him. Phlegyas, whose father was Mars (god of war), appears in Virgil's underworld as an admonition against showing contempt for the gods (*Aeneid* 6.618–20). Megaera, one of the Furies (see entry below), tortures a famished and irritable Phlegyas in Statius's *Thebaid* (1.712–15).

FILIPPO ARGENTI (8) :: Apart from what transpires in *Inferno* 8.31–63, we know little of the hotheaded character who quarrels with Dante, lays his hands on the boat (to capsize it?), and is finally torn to pieces by his wrathful cohorts. Early commentators report that his name derived from an ostentatious habit of shoeing his horse in silver (*argento*). A black Guelph, Filippo was Dante's natural political enemy, but the tone of the episode suggests personal animosity as well. Some try to explain Dante's harsh treatment of Filippo as payback for a supposed earlier offense—namely, Filippo once slapped Dante in the face, or Filippo's brother took possession of Dante's confiscated property after the poet had been exiled from Florence. Boccaccio, in *Decameron* 9.8, highlights Filippo's violent temper by having the character throttle a man who is tricked—by a glutton named CIACCO (Circle 3)—into crossing him.

FALLEN ANGELS (8) :: Dante's fallen angels—they literally "rained down from Heaven" (*Inf.* 8.82–83)—defend the city of Dis (Lower Hell), just as they once resisted Christ's arrival at the GATE OF HELL (Periphery of Hell). These angels joined Lucifer in his rebellion against God; cast out of Heaven, they laid the foundation for evil in the world. Once beautiful, they are now, like all things infernal, transformed into monstrous demons. Virgil previously described the HARROWING

OF HELL (Circle 1) in *Inferno* 4.52–63. He now alludes to a specific effect of the Harrowing—damage to the gate of Hell—in noting the arrogance of the demons at the entrance to Dis (*Inf.* 8.124–26).

FURIES (AND MEDUSA) (9) :: With the appearance of the three Furies, who threaten to call on Medusa, Virgil's credibility and Dante's survival appear to be at risk. Virgil is exceptionally animated as he directs Dante's attention to the Furies (also called Erinyes, Eumenides, or Dirae) and identifies each one by name: Megaera, Tisiphone, and Allecto (*Inf.* 9.45–48). This is a moment in the journey when Virgil's legacy as the author of his own epic poem, in which he himself writes of such creatures as the Furies and Medusa, is central to the meaning of Dante's episode. The Furies, according to Virgil's classical world, were a terrifying trio of "daughters of Night"—bloodstained, with snakes in their hair and about their waists—who were often invoked to exact revenge on behalf of offended mortals and gods. DIDO (Circle 2, "Famous Lovers"), distraught upon seeing Aeneas sail off from Carthage, calls on the avenging Furies (along with other deities) to bring suffering to the fleeing Trojan and his comrades and to instill lasting enmity between their two peoples (*Aeneid* 4.607–29). One Fury, Allecto, is summoned by Juno to instigate warfare between the Trojans and the Italian natives (*Aeneid* 7.323–571), and an unspecified member of the trio is sent by Jupiter finally to resolve the conflict in favor of the Trojans: she does so by depriving the Italian hero TURNUS (Dark Wood, "Greyhound Prophecy") of his protectress and his strength, thus enabling Aeneas to vanquish him (*Aeneid* 12.843–952).

Ovid tells how Minerva, offended that Neptune and Medusa made love in the goddess's temple, punishes the beautiful girl by transforming her lovely hair into snakes. Medusa, one of three sisters known as the Gorgons, thus becomes so frightening to behold that those who look at her turn to stone. The Greek hero Perseus, aided by a bronze shield in which he can see Medusa's reflected image (rather than looking directly at her), kills her as she sleeps by cutting off her head. Pegasus, the winged horse, is born of Medusa's blood (*Metamorphoses* 4.772–803). Representations of Perseus holding aloft the horrible head of Medusa were common in the early modern period. A Renaissance sculpture of the scene, by Cellini, has for many years decked the loggia in Piazza della Signoria, one of the main squares in Florence. The fact that, in the Middle Ages, the Furies and Medusa were commonly thought to signify various evils (or components of sin), from obstinacy and doubt to heresy and pride, may help to explain the travelers' difficulties at the entrance to Dis. Early commentators draw on etymological associations of the Furies' names—evil thought (Allecto), evil words (Tisiphone), evil deeds (Megaera)—to describe stages and manifestations of sin (often with an emphasis on heresy) that can turn people to stone by making them "obstinate cultivators of earthly things" (Boccaccio).

HEAVEN'S MESSENGER (9) :: Although Virgil anticipated the arrival of the messenger from Heaven (*Inf.* 8.128–30, 9.8–9), who rebukes the demons so that the travelers may enter Dis (Lower Hell), the being is never precisely identified. Literally "sent from Heaven" (*Inf.* 9.85), he supports both classical and Christian interpretations in his appearance and actions. As an enemy of Hell who walks on water (*Inf.* 9.81) and opens the gates of Dis as Christ once opened the gate of Hell (*Inf.* 8.124–30, 9.89–90), the messenger is certainly Christlike. He also bears similarities to Hermes-Mercury, the classical god who, borne on winged feet, delivers messages to mortals from the heavens. The little wand of the heavenly messenger (*Inf.* 9.89) recalls the caduceus, the staff with which Hermes-Mercury guides souls of the dead to Hades. Both Christ and Hermes were strongly associated with the kind of allegory Dante describes in *Inferno* 9.61–63—specifically, the idea that a deeper meaning lies hidden beneath the surface meaning of words (see "Allegory" below).

Allusions

WRATH AND SULLENNESS (7–8) :: Like the fourth circle of Hell, circle five (presented in *Inferno* 7 and 8) contains two related groups of sinners. But whereas avarice and prodigality are distinct sins based on the same principle (an immoderate attitude toward material wealth), wrath and sullenness are basically two forms of a single sin: anger that is expressed (wrath) and anger that is repressed (sullenness). This idea that anger takes various forms is common in ancient and medieval thought. The two groups suffer different punishments appropriate to their type of anger: the wrathful ruthlessly attack one another while the sullen stew below the surface of the muddy swamp (*Inf.* 7.109–26), even as they are all confined to Styx.

DIS (8–9) :: Dante designates all of Lower Hell—circles six through nine, where more serious sins are punished—as the walled city of Dis (*Inf.* 8.68), one of the names for the king of the classical underworld (Pluto) and, by extension, the underworld in general. For Dante, then, Dis stands both for Lucifer and the lower circles of his infernal realm. It may be significant that Virgil, who repeatedly refers to Dis in his *Aeneid* (e.g., 4.702, 5.731, 6.127, 6.269), is the one who announces the travelers' approach to Dis in the *Divine Comedy*. Details of the city and its surroundings in *Inferno* 8 and 9—including moats, watchtowers, high walls, and a well-guarded entrance—suggest a citizenry ready for battle.

STYX (7–8) :: The Styx is a body of water (a marsh or river) in the classical underworld. Virgil describes it in his *Aeneid* as the marsh across which Charon ferries souls of the dead (and the living Aeneas) into the lower world (*Aeneid* 6.384–416). Dante's presentation of the infernal waterways—and the topography of the otherworld in general—is much more detailed and precise (and therefore more realistic and recognizable) than the descriptions of his classical and medieval precursors. The Styx, according to Dante's design, is a vast swamp encompassing the fifth circle of Hell, in which the wrathful and sullen are punished. It also serves a practical purpose in the journey when Dante and Virgil are taken by Phlegyas in his swift vessel across the marsh to the city of Dis. Because Dante is present in the flesh (unlike the shades in the afterlife), his weight causes Phlegyas's craft to travel lower in the water (*Inf.* 8.25–30). Virgil notes a similar effect in the *Aeneid* (6.412–16) when Aeneas boards the vessel piloted by Charon.

THESEUS AND HERCULES (9) :: The heavenly messenger pointedly reminds the demons at the entrance to Dis that Dante will not be the first living man to breach their walls. Theseus and Hercules, two classical heroes (each has a divine parent), previously raided the underworld and returned alive. Hercules, in fact, descended into Hades to rescue Theseus, who had been imprisoned following his unsuccessful attempt to abduct Persephone, queen of Hades. While the Furies express regret at not having killed Theseus when they had the chance (*Inf.* 9.54), the heavenly messenger recalls that CERBERUS (Circle 3) bore the brunt of Hercules' fury, as he was dragged by his chain along the hard floor of the underworld (*Inf.* 9.97–99). In Virgil's epic CHARON (Periphery of Hell) tries to dissuade Aeneas from boarding his boat by voicing his displeasure at having already transported Hercules and Theseus to the underworld (*Aeneid* 6.392–97).

ERICHTHO (9) :: Dante's desire to know whether anyone has previously made the journey from Upper to Lower Hell is evidence of the psychologically complex relationship that develops between the two travelers during their time together (*Inf.* 9.16–18). Given the impasse at the entrance to Dis, Dante understandably wants to know, as his question not so subtly implies, if his guide is up to the task. Virgil's savvy response that, yes, he himself has once before made such a journey, is his way of saying, "Don't worry, I know what I'm doing!" Virgil's story, that he was summoned by Erichtho to retrieve a soul from the lowest circle of Hell (*Inf.* 9.25–30), is Dante's invention. The poet Dante thus invents a story so that Virgil can save face and reassure the character Dante. The poet likely based this story on a gruesome episode from Lucan's *Pharsalia* (6.507–830): Erichtho, a bloodthirsty witch, calls back from the underworld the shade of a freshly killed soldier so that he can reveal future events in the civil war between Pompey and Caesar. By making Virgil a victim of Erichtho's sorcery, Dante draws on the popular belief, widespread in the Middle Ages, that Virgil himself possessed magical, prophetic powers.

ALLEGORY (9) :: When Dante interrupts the narrative to instruct his (smart) readers to "note the doctrine hidden under the veil of the strange verses" (*Inf.* 9.61–63), he calls upon the popular medieval tradition of allegorical reading. Commonly applied to the interpretation of sacred texts (namely, the Bible), allegory, in its various forms, assumes that other, deeper levels of meaning (often spiritual) lie beneath the surface in addition to (or in place of) the literal meaning of the words. Allegory was also used to "moralize" (or Christianize) classical works, such as Ovid's *Metamorphoses*. The medieval Platonic tradition often allegorically interpreted texts according to a body of esoteric doctrine believed to originate with Hermes (hence "hermeticism").

Significant Verses

> Tutti gridavano: "A Filippo Argenti!" (*Inf.* 8.61)
> *They all yelled out: "Get Filippo Argenti!"*

> sotto 'l velame de li versi strani (*Inf.* 9.63)
> *under the veil of the strange verses*

Study Questions

1 :: How would you describe Dante's behavior and attitude toward Filippo Argenti? Why is this reaction, so different from Dante's earlier responses to Francesca and Ciacco, appropriate here?

2 :: Why do you think Virgil is unable to overcome on his own the resistance of the demons at the entrance to Dis?

3 :: How might Virgil's difficulties (and their resolution) relate to the teaching that is hidden "under the veil of the strange verses" (*Inf.* 9.63)?

Circle 6: Heresy

INFERNO 9–11

AFTER PASSING THROUGH the walls of Dis, Virgil leads Dante across the sixth circle of Hell, a vast plain resembling a cemetery. Stone tombs, raised above the ground with their lids removed, glow red from the heat of flames. Buried in these sepulchers are the souls of heretics, each tomb holding an untold number of individuals who adhered to a particular doctrine but who are all punished according to the broadest notion of heresy: denial of the soul's immortality. Dante sees standing upright in one tomb the imposing figure of Farinata, a Florentine leader of the Ghibellines, the political party bitterly opposed to the party of Dante's ancestors. Peering out from the same tomb is the father of Dante's best friend; Cavalcante is upset that his son Guido is not with Dante on the journey. Here Dante learns, as the result of a misunderstanding, that the damned possess the power to see the future but not the present. Needing time to adjust to the stench wafting up from lower circles, the travelers take refuge behind the tomb of a heretical pope. Virgil uses this time to describe the overall layout of Hell and the reasons for this organization.

Encounters

FARINATA (10) :: Farinata degli Uberti, one of the Florentine men of worth whose fate Dante sought to learn from CIACCO (Circle 3), cuts an imposing figure—rising out of his burning tomb "from the waist up" and seeming to "have great contempt for Hell"—when Dante turns to address him in the circle of the heretics (*Inf.* 10.31–36). His very first question to Dante, "Who were your ancestors?" (*Inf.* 10.42), reveals the tight relationship between family and politics in thirteenth-century Italy. As a Florentine leader of the Ghibellines, Farinata was an enemy to the Guelphs, the party of Dante's ancestors. Farinata's Ghibellines twice defeated the Guelphs (in 1248 and 1260), but both times the Guelphs succeeded in returning to power; the Ghibellines, however, failed to rise again following their defeat in 1266. Farinata's family (the Uberti) was explicitly excluded from later amnesties (he had died in 1264), and in 1283 he and his wife (both posthumously charged with heresy) were excommunicated, their bodies disinterred and burned, and the possessions of their heirs confiscated. These politically motivated wars and vendettas, in which victors banished their adversaries, literally divided Florence's populace. While there is certainly no love lost between Dante and Farinata, there is a measure of respect. Farinata, called *magnanimo*—"greathearted"—by the narrator (*Inf.* 10.73), put Florence above politics when he stood up to his victorious colleagues and argued against destroying the city completely (*Inf.* 10.91–93).

Farinata identifies only two of the many heretical shades (over a thousand) with whom he shares his tomb, the "second Frederick" and the "Cardinal" (*Inf.* 10.118–20). Emperor **Frederick II** was important to Dante as last in the line of reigning Holy Roman Emperors. Raised in Palermo, in the Kingdom of Sicily, Frederick was crowned emperor in Rome in 1220. A central figure in the conflict between the empire and the papacy (see "Guelphs and Ghibellines" below), he was twice excommunicated (1227 and 1239) and finally deposed (1245) before his death in 1250. In placing Frederick among the heretics, Dante is likely following the accusations of the emperor's enemies. Elsewhere Dante praises Frederick, along with his son Manfred, as a paragon of nobility and integrity (*De vulgari eloquentia* 1.12.4). Frederick's court at Palermo was known as an intellectual and cultural capital, with fruitful interactions among talented individuals—philosophers, artists, musicians, scientists, and poets—from Italian, Latin, northern European, Muslim, Jewish, and Greek traditions. Frederick's court nourished the first major movement in Italian vernacular poetry; this so-called Sicilian School, in which the sonnet was first developed, contributed greatly to the establishment of the Italian literary tradition that influenced the young Dante.

The "Cardinal" is widely believed to be **Cardinal Ottaviano degli Ubaldini**, a precocious and powerful church leader; made bishop of Bologna before he turned thirty (by special dispensation of Pope Gregory IX), Ottaviano attained the rank of cardinal four years later, in 1244. He died in 1273. Despite his prominent position in the church, he was known as a strong protector and proponent of the Ghibelline (or imperial) party. One early commentator relates how Ottaviano, irate when Tuscan Ghibellines denied him a sum of money he needed for a project, declared: "If the soul exists, I have lost mine a thousand times for the Ghibellines" (Benvenuto).

CAVALCANTE DE' CAVALCANTI (10) :: Whereas Farinata is an intimidating presence, standing in his tomb and towering above his interlocutor, Cavalcante de' Cavalcanti lifts only his head above the edge of the same tomb. A member of a rich and powerful Guelph family, Cavalcante, like Dante's ancestors, was an enemy to Farinata and the Ghibellines. To help bridge the Guelph-Ghibelline divide, Cavalcante married his son (see "Guido Cavalcanti" below) to Farinata's daughter (Beatrice degli Uberti). Whereas Farinata is primarily concerned with politics, Cavalcante is obsessed with the fate of his son (*Inf.* 10.58–72), whom Dante in another work calls his best friend (*Vita nuova* 3.14). Cavalcante's alleged heresy may be more a matter of guilt by association with his son's worldview than a reflection of his own spiritual beliefs.

POPE ANASTASIUS (11) :: To shield themselves from the awful stench rising from the circles below, Dante and Virgil huddle behind a stone tomb cover that bears the inscription, "I hold Pope Anastasius, whom Photinus drew from the straight way" (*Inf.* 11.8–9). Anastasius II, an early medieval pontiff (496–98), was considered a heretic by later generations for having been persuaded by Photinus (a deacon of Thessalonica) to support the efforts of a contemporary emperor of the same name (Anastasius I) to restore the reputation of Acacius, a patriarch of Constantinople who denied the divine origin of Christ. Pope Anastasius II was punished by God for his heretical error, according to several early commentators (L'Ottimo, Anonimo Fiorentino), by suffering a miserable end: when he sat down to defecate, his internal organs spilled out and he died.

Allusions

HERESY :: Dante opts for the most generic conception of heresy—the denial of the soul's immortality (*Inf.* 10.15)—perhaps in deference to the spiritual and philosophical positions of specific characters he wishes to feature here, or perhaps for the opportunity to present an especially effective form of *contrapasso:* heretical souls eternally tormented in fiery tombs. More commonly, heresy in the Middle Ages was a product of acrimonious disputes over Christian doctrine, in particular the theologically correct ways of understanding the Trinity and Christ. Crusades were waged against "heretical sects," and individuals accused of other crimes or sins (such as witchcraft, usury, and sodomy) were frequently labeled heretics as well.

Heresy, according to a theological argument based on the dividing of Jesus's tunic by Roman soldiers (Matthew 27:35), was traditionally viewed as an act of division, a symbolic laceration in the community of "true" believers. This may help explain why divisive, partisan politics is such a prominent theme in Dante's encounter with Farinata. Umberto Eco's best-selling novel *The Name of the Rose* (1980), set in a northern Italian monastery only a few decades after the time of Dante's poem (and made into a film in 1986), provides a learned and entertaining portrayal of heretics and their persecutors.

EPICURUS (10) :: Epicurus was a Greek philosopher (341–270 BCE) who espoused the doctrine that pleasure—defined in terms of serenity, the absence of pain and passion—is the highest human good. By identifying the heretics as followers of Epicurus (*Inf.* 10.13–14), Dante condemns the Epicurean idea that the soul, like the body, is mortal. In Latin literature, this view is best represented by Lucretius's *De rerum natura* (*On the Nature of Things*), a text not known directly by Dante.

GUIDO CAVALCANTI (10) :: Dante's best friend, Guido Cavalcanti, a few years older than Dante, was an aristocratic white Guelph and an erudite, accomplished poet in his own right. Guido's best-known poem, "Donna me prega" ("A lady asks me"), is a stylistically sophisticated example of his philosophical view of love as a dark force that leads one to misery and often to death. When Dante says that Guido perhaps "held in disdain" someone connected with his journey (*Inf.* 10.63), the past tense may mean that Guido (who is still alive) failed to appreciate Beatrice's spiritual importance at some earlier point in time (she died in 1290). Guido's father, in any case, takes this past tense to mean that his son is already dead. While the character Dante knows that Guido is living at the time of the journey (March–April 1300), the poet Dante knows he will not live much longer. Worse still, he knows that he is partly, if indirectly, responsible for the death of his friend in August 1300. As one of the priors of Florence (June 15–August 15, 1300), Dante joined in a decision to punish both parties (white and black Guelphs) for recent fighting by banishing their ringleaders, one of whom was Guido Cavalcanti. Tragically, Guido fell ill due to the bad climate of the region to which he was sent (he likely contracted malaria) and died shortly after his return to Florence.

GUELPHS AND GHIBELLINES (10) :: While the Florentine political parties at the time of Dante's journey were the WHITE AND BLACK GUELPHS (Circle 3, "Florentine Politics"), the city had, before Dante's childhood, participated in the political struggle between Guelphs and Ghibellines, a more general conflict that raged throughout the Italian peninsular and in other parts of Europe. Derived from two warring royal houses in Germany (Welf and Waiblingen), the sides came to be distinguished by their adherence to the claims of the pope (Guelphs) or the emperor (Ghibellines). For a time, Florence alternated between Guelph and Ghibelline rule. Ghibelline forces from Siena and Florence, led by FARINATA and others, scored a devastating victory over Florentine Guelphs at the battle of Montaperti (near Siena) in 1260, but the Guelph cause finally triumphed with the death of Manfred, son of Emperor FREDERICK II (see "Farinata" above), at the battle of Benevento (in southern Italy) in 1266. Guelph Florence cemented its dominance in Tuscany in 1289, when its army defeated Ghibelline forces from Arezzo at the battle of Campaldino. The struggle in Florence began, according to medieval chronicles, with a clash between two prominent families and their allies in 1215 or 1216: young Buondelmonte de' Buondelmonti, the story goes, was murdered by the Amidei and their supporters on Easter Sunday after he broke his promise to marry an Amidei woman (as part of a peace arrangement) and wed one of the Donati instead. This event came to be seen as the origin of factional violence that would plague the city for the next century and beyond.

HYPEROPIA (10) :: We learn from Farinata that the heretics, and apparently all the damned, possess the supernatural ability to "see" future events (*Inf.* 10.94–108). However, like those who suffer from hyperopia ("farsightedness"), their visual acuity decreases as events come closer to the present. Because there will no longer be a future when the world ends (LAST JUDGMENT [Circle 3]), souls of the damned will thereafter have no external awareness to distract them from their eternal suffering.

MORAL STRUCTURE OF HELL (11) :: Needing to adjust to the smell rising from the bottom three circles of Hell, Virgil and Dante delay their descent. Virgil makes good use of this time by explaining how Hell is organized according to different types of sin. Here we see that Dante's syncretic use of multiple sources or systems produces an original (if messy) moral conception of Hell. The poet's overall structure appears to derive from the tripartite Aristotelian classification, as mediated by

Thomas Aquinas, of negative character qualities (*Nichomachean Ethics* 7.1.1145a): "incontinence," "mad bestiality" ("brutishness" is the more common translation of Aristotle's term), and "malice." Commentators often relate these three categories to the THREE BEASTS that threaten Dante in the dark wood. These "three dispositions that Heaven rejects," as Virgil puts it (*Inf.* 11.79–81), correspond to the concupiscent, rational, and irascible appetites in the human soul, and therefore to the three major divisions of Dante's Hell: sins of incontinence (circles two through five), sins of violence (circle seven), and sins of fraud (circles eight and nine). Because fraud is unique to humans, Virgil says that sins of fraud are worse than sins of violence (*Inf.* 11.25–27), which accords with Cicero's view (*On Duty* 1.13.41). Virgil further explains, following Aristotle, that incontinence, which is excessive indulgence of desires deemed good in themselves, is punished in the upper circles of Hell because it is the least offensive type of sin (*Inf.* 11.83–90). To define usury as a violent sin against the Godhead (like blasphemy and sodomy), Virgil draws first on Aristotle's *Physics* (to establish human labor as the offspring of nature and thus the grandchild of God) and then on the Bible (Genesis 3:17–19), which ordains that humankind must earn its way in the world through nature and labor (*Inf.* 11.106–8).

Two complications arise from Virgil's exposition of the moral structure of Hell. First, his scheme appears to have no place for the heretics, the souls in Limbo, and the cowardly opportunists punished inside the gate of Hell but before the river Acheron; this is perhaps due to the fact that these "faults," since their source is not in the will (the three-part appetite) but in the intellect, are the result of *not* doing something or *not* believing in or worshiping God (or not worshiping correctly). Second, the term *malizia* ("malice") is used in two apparently contradictory ways: Virgil first says that malice is the cause of injury or injustice, either through force or through fraud (*Inf.* 11.22–24), while he later lists malice, incontinence, and mad bestiality as the three sinful dispositions (*Inf.* 11.81–83). Does violence, then, correspond to the malicious use of force (as the first passage suggests) or does it correspond to mad bestiality (as the second passage suggests)? This may just be a case, not uncommon in medieval thought, where the same word (*malizia*) has both a generic meaning (rational evildoing, by force or by fraud) and a more specific meaning (fraud alone). The author of the "Letter to Can

Grande" (possibly Dante himself) similarly uses the word *allegory* in both a broad sense (having a meaning different from the literal or historical meaning) and a specific sense (what one believes).

Significant Verses

che l'anima col corpo morta fanno (*Inf.* 10.15)
who make the soul die with the body

Vedi là Farinata che s'è dritto (*Inf.* 10.32)
Look there at Farinata who has stood up

forse cui Guido vostro ebbe a disdegno (*Inf.* 10.63)
to someone whom perhaps your Guido held in disdain

Study Questions

1 :: Explain the *contrapasso* in circle six based on Dante's conception of heresy as denial of the immortality of the soul (*Inf.* 10.15).

2 :: What does it say about Dante, himself an exiled victim of partisan politics, that he presents Farinata as both a political enemy and a defender of Florence?

3 :: Why does Dante's use of the past tense in *Inferno* 10.63 ("held in disdain") cause Cavalcante such grief? And why is Dante then confused by this reaction?

4 :: How does Dante's treatment of his friend, Guido Cavalcanti, in *Inferno* 10 perhaps reflect his relationship with Guido in real life?

Circle 7: Violence

INFERNO 12–17

AFTER SLIPPING BY the Minotaur, Dante and Virgil visit the three areas of circle seven, where the violent shades are punished. Astride the Centaur Nessus, Dante views those who committed violent acts against fellow human beings, from ruthless tyrants and warriors (such as Attila the Hun) to murderers and highway bandits, all submerged to an appropriate depth in a river of boiling blood. The travelers then enter a foreboding forest whose gnarled and stunted trees are the souls of suicides. Harpies inflict pain on the suicide-trees by feeding on their leaves, while the wounds created by the Harpies' gnawing provide an outlet for this pain. Here Dante is moved by the tale of Pier della Vigna, a high-ranking official brought to ruin by envious rivals at court, and he sees men who squandered their wealth chased and dismembered by ferocious black dogs. Dante and Virgil next cross a desert scorched by a rain of fire punishing violent offenders against God: blasphemers flat on their backs (including Capaneus, a defiant classical warrior); sodomites in continuous movement (among these Brunetto Latini, Dante's beloved teacher); and usurers crouching on the ground with purses, decorated with their families' coats of arms, hanging from their necks. Dante and Virgil descend to the next circle aboard Geryon, a creature with a human face, reptilian body, and scorpion's tail.

Encounters

MINOTAUR (12) :: The path down to the three rings of circle seven is covered with a mass of boulders that fell, as Virgil explains (*Inf.* 12.31–45), during the earthquake triggered by Christ's HARROWING OF HELL (Circle 1; see also Circle 5, "Fallen Angels"). The Minotaur, a bull-man who appears on this broken slope (*Inf.* 12.11–15), is most likely a guardian and symbol of the entire circle of violence. Basic information on the Minotaur was available to Dante from Virgil (*Aeneid* 6.20–30; *Eclogue* 6.45–60) and Ovid (*Metamorphoses* 8.131–73; *Heroides* 10.101–2; *Art of Love* 1.289–326), with additional details provided by medieval commentators (such as Pseudo-Bernardus Silvestris and William of Conches). Dante does not specify whether the Minotaur has a man's head and bull's body or the other way around (sources support both possibilities), but he underscores the bestial rage of the hybrid creature. At the sight of Dante and Virgil, the Minotaur bites himself, and his frenzied bucking, set off by Virgil's mention of the monster's executioner, allows the travelers to proceed unharmed. Almost everything about the Minotaur's story, from his creation to his demise, contains some form of violence. Pasiphaë, wife of King MINOS of Crete (Circle 2), lusted after a beautiful white bull and asked Daedalus to construct a "fake cow" (*Inf.* 12.13) in which she could conceal herself to induce the bull to mate with her; Daedalus obliged and the Minotaur was conceived. Minos wisely had Daedalus build an elaborate labyrinth to conceal and contain this monstrosity. To punish the Athenians, who had killed his son (Androgeos), Minos supplied the Minotaur each year (or every nine years; Ovid, *Metamorphoses* 8.171) with a sacrificial offering of Athenian youth, seven boys and seven girls. When Ariadne (the Minotaur's half-sister; *Inf.* 12.20) fell in love with one of these boys (THESEUS [Circle 5]; *Inf.* 12.16–18), the two of them devised a plan to slay the Minotaur: Theseus entered the labyrinth with a sword (or club; Ovid, *Heroides* 10.101–2) and a ball of thread, which he unwound as he proceeded toward the center; having slain the Minotaur, Theseus was thus able to retrace his steps and escape the labyrinth.

CENTAURS (12) :: The Centaurs, men from the waist up with the lower bodies of horses, guard the first ring of circle seven, a river of blood in which the shades of tyrants, murderers, and bandits are plunged. Armed with bows and arrows, thousands of Centaurs patrol the bank of the river, using their weapons to keep the souls submerged to a depth commensurate with their culpability (*Inf.* 12.73–75). In classical mythology, the Centaurs are perhaps best known for their uncouth, violent behavior: guests at a wedding, they attempted (their lust incited by wine) to carry off the bride and other women; a fierce battle ensued, described by Ovid in all its gory detail (*Metamorphoses* 12.210–535), in which the horse-men suffered the heaviest losses, including several brutal deaths at the hands of THESEUS (see "Minotaur" above). Two of the three Centaurs who approach Dante and Virgil fully earned this negative reputation. **Pholus**, whom Virgil describes as "full of rage" (*Inf.* 12.72), was one of the combatants at the wedding. **Nessus**, selected to carry Dante across the river in Hell, was killed by HERCULES (Circle 5) with a poisoned arrow for attempting to rape the hero's beautiful wife, Deianira, after Hercules had entrusted the Centaur to carry her across a river. Nessus avenged his own death: he gave his blood-soaked shirt to Deianira as a "love charm," which she, not knowing it was poisoned, later gave to Hercules when she doubted his love (*Inf.* 12.67–69; Ovid, *Metamorphoses* 9.101–272). **Chiron**, leader of the Centaurs, enjoyed a more favorable reputation as the wise tutor of both Hercules and Achilles (*Inf.* 12.71).

TYRANTS, MURDERERS, HIGHWAY ROBBERS (12) :: The Centaur Nessus identifies the shades of several notoriously violent tyrants and criminals, who are submerged to varying depths in the river of boiling blood. Only the tops of the tyrants' heads are visible. **Alexander the Great** (356–323 BCE), king of Macedonia, whom Dante elsewhere praises as an example of munificence (*Convivio* 4.11.14) and as a ruler who nearly attained universal sovereignty (*Monarchia* 2.8.8), suffers here for his reputation (promulgated by Dante's chief sources for ancient history) as a cruel, bloodthirsty man who inflicted great harm on the world (Orosius, *History* 3.7.5, 3.18.10; Lucan, *Pharsalia* 10.20–36). Nessus pairs Alexander with Dionysius (*Inf.* 12.106–8), most likely **Dionysius the Elder**, known as the tyrant of Syracuse (Sicily) for his harsh treatment of his subjects over nearly forty years (405–367 BCE). Similarly paired are two Italian warlords (*Inf.* 12.109–12): **Ezzelino da Romano** (1194–1259), son-in-law of FREDERICK II (Circle 6) and leader of the Ghibellines in northern Italy, was so ruthless and feared—he was reported to have had eleven thousand Paduans burned to death in one massacre (Villani, *Chronicle* 7.72)—that Pope Alexander IV, calling Ezzelino "the most inhuman of the children of men," launched a crusade against him in 1255. Dark-featured and hairy, Ezzelino is reported by one early commentator to have sported a single hair on his nose; when he became angry, this hair stood straight up, causing those around him to flee (Benvenuto). The blond head next to Ezzelino belongs to **Obizzo da Este** (1247–93), a Guelph nobleman from Ferrara who also ruled other cities in north-central Italy; known for his cruelty, Obizzo himself became a victim of violence when his son (Dante says "stepson," perhaps to emphasize the wickedness of the crime) smothered him with a pillow. Among the murderers, submerged up to their necks in the hot blood, is **Guy de Montfort**, an English nobleman who, to avenge the death of his father, killed his cousin, Prince Henry of Cornwall, with a sword; the murder took place in Viterbo (a city north of Rome) during a Mass in 1271 (supposedly while Henry, as the priest raised the Host, was on his knees); following Villani (*Chronicle* 8.39), Dante has Nessus say that the heart of the slain prince, preserved in a gold cup and placed on a column of London Bridge, still drips blood into the River Thames (*Inf.* 12.118–20).

Nessus names five additional perpetrators of violence against others, who are not seen by Dante because they are located at a distance from the shallow point where the Centaur carries him across the river of blood (*Inf.* 12.133–38). So feared was **Attila**, king of the Huns (ruled 434–53), in his conquests of eastern and western portions of the Roman Empire that he was called *Flagellum Dei* ("Scourge of God"); Dante undoubtedly found Attila even more despicable because of a mistaken belief that he had destroyed Florence in 440 (*Inf.* 13.149). **Pyrrhus**, according to some commentators, is the king of Epirus (lived 319–272 BCE) who twice invaded Italy to wage war against the Romans. Others believe he is the son of Achilles, infamous for his cruelty when the Greeks destroyed Troy; this Pyrrhus killed the Trojan prince Polites before the very eyes of his parents (Priam and Hecuba), and then dragged King Priam to the altar, where he killed him as well (Virgil, *Aeneid* 2.526–53). **Sextus** likely refers to the son of Pompey the Great, who, following the murder of Julius Caesar, took over a fleet and, using Sicily as a base, caused havoc along the coasts of Italy—hence earning the title of "Sicilian pirate" (Lucan, *Pharsalia* 6.422)—before he was captured by Augustus's troops (under Agrippa) and executed. **Rinier da Corneto** and **Rinier Pazzo** were notorious highwaymen of thirteenth-century Italy, the former harassing travelers on the roads to Rome, the latter operating between Florence and Arezzo. Rinier Pazzo was excommunicated by Pope Clement IV and outlawed by the Florentine commune (which put a price on his head) for one of his most spectacular crimes: in 1268 he led a group of bandits that robbed a bishop and his entourage as they headed for Rome, slaughtering nearly all of them.

HARPIES (13) :: The Harpies, foul creatures with women's heads and birds' bodies, are perched in the suicide-trees, whose leaves they tear and eat, thus producing both pain and an outlet for the accompanying laments of the souls (*Inf.* 13.13–15, 101–2). Harpies, as Dante (the narrator) recalls (*Inf.* 13.10–12), play a small but noteworthy role in Aeneas's voyage from Troy to Italy. Newly arrived on the Strophades (islands in the Ionian sea), Aeneas and his crew slaughter cattle and goats and prepare the meat for a sumptuous feast. Twice the horrid Harpies, who inhabit the islands after being driven from their previous feeding location, spoil the banquet by falling upon the food and fouling the area with repugnant excretions. The Trojans meet a third attack with their weapons and succeed in driving away the Harpies. However, Celaeno, a Harpy with the gift of prophecy, in turn drives away the Trojans when she announces they will not accomplish their mission in Italy without suffering such terrible hunger that they are forced to eat their tables (Virgil, *Aeneid* 3.209–67). The Trojans in fact realize their journey is over when they eat the bread—that is, the "table"—upon which they have heaped other food gathered from the Italian countryside (*Aeneid* 7.112–22).

PIER DELLA VIGNA (13) :: Like Dante, Pier della Vigna (ca. 1190–1249) was an accomplished poet (part of the Sicilian School, he wrote sonnets) and a victim of his own faithful service to the state. With a first-rate legal education and ample rhetorical talent, Pier rose quickly through the ranks of public service in the Kingdom of Sicily, from scribe and notary to judge and official spokesman for the imperial court of FREDERICK II (Circle 6). But his powers appear to have exceeded even these titles, as Pier claims to have had final say over Frederick's decisions (*Inf.* 13.58–63). While evidence of corruption casts some doubt on Pier's account of faithful service to the emperor, it is generally believed that he was indeed falsely accused of betraying Frederick's trust by envious colleagues and political enemies (*Inf.* 13.64–69). In this way, his story recalls that of BOETHIUS (Circle 4, "Fortuna"), author of *Consolation of Philosophy,* a well-known book in the Middle Ages (and a favorite of Dante) recounting the fall from power of another talented individual falsely accused of betraying his emperor. Early commentators say that Frederick, believing the charges against Pier (perhaps that he had plotted with the pope against the emperor), had him imprisoned and blinded. Unable to accept this wretched fate, Pier brutally took his own life by smashing his head against a wall (perhaps the wall of a church) or (in other accounts) by leaping from a high window as the emperor was passing in the street below.

Pier's name (*Vigna* means "vineyard") undoubtedly made him an even more attractive candidate for Dante's suicide-trees. As an added part of the *contrapasso,* Dante learns the souls of the suicides will not be reunited with their bodies at the LAST JUDGMENT (Circle 3; see also Circle 6, "Hyperopia"); instead, their retrieved corpses will hang on the trees (*Inf.* 13.103–8).

SQUANDERERS AND ANONYMOUS FLORENTINE SUI-
CIDE (13) :: Chased through the wood of the suicide-trees by a
pack of swift black dogs are two men damned to this region of Hell for
setting violent hands on their own possessions. The one in front, who
calls on death to come quickly (*Inf.* 13.118) but for now manages to elude
the dogs, is Arcolano ("**Lano**") di Squarcia Maconi. Part of a group of
rich, young Sienese men known as the Spendthrift Club (Brigata Spen-
dereccia), Lano went through his wealth so quickly that he was soon
reduced to poverty. When, during a military campaign against Arezzo,
the Sienese troops were caught in an ambush at the Pieve del Toppo,
Lano basically chose to die (even though he could have saved himself)
rather than face up to the problems caused by his self-destructive im-
pulses. The slower man, who reminds Lano of his death at the ambush
(*Inf.* 13.120–21), is identified by the bush into which he collapses as **Iacopo da Santo Andrea**. His shade-body is torn apart by the ferocious
dogs (*Inf.* 13.127–29), much as he himself tore through his considerable
resources. Iacopo, said to have been the wealthiest private citizen in
Padua, was known for senseless acts of dissoluteness, such as throw-
ing money into a river during a boat ride (so as not to appear idle) and
setting fire to all the cottages on his estate to provide a spectacular welcome for a group of important dinner guests (Benvenuto). EZZELINO
DA ROMANO, one of the tyrants punished in the river of blood (above),
had Iacopo executed in 1239.

The suicide-bush that suffers broken branches from Iacopo's tum-
ble and dismemberment never gives his name but identifies himself as
a citizen of Florence. Some commentators think he is Lotto degli Agli
(a judge who took his life after delivering an unjust verdict) or Rocco
de' Mozzi, who killed himself after his business failed and he lost his
wealth. It is also possible that this **anonymous suicide**, who says he
hanged himself in his own home (*Inf.* 13.151), represents the entire
city of Florence instead of (or in addition to) a particular individual:
when Florence, according to legend, expressed its emerging Christian
identity in the fourth century by adopting John the Baptist as its patron saint (in place of Mars, its first patron), the city destined itself
to face the bellicose god's retribution in the form of factional violence.
Chroniclers report that a statue of Mars, which fell into the Arno during the destruction of Florence in 450, was fished out of the river when

the city was rebuilt under Charlemagne in the early ninth century (*Inf.* 13.143–50). A statue, thought to be of Mars, that did in fact exist in the Florence of Dante's day was swept away in the great flood of 1333. Dante's declaration of love for Florence as his motivation for gathering scattered branches of the suicide-bush (*Inf.* 14.1–3) reinforces the identification of this anonymous suicide with the poet's native city.

CAPANEUS (14) :: A huge and powerful warrior-king who virtually embodies defiance against his highest god, Capaneus is an exemplary blasphemer—with blasphemy understood as direct violence against God. Still, it is striking that Dante selects a pagan character to represent one of the few specifically religious sins punished in Hell.

Dante's portrayal of Capaneus in *Inferno* 14.43–72 (his large size and scornful account of Jove striking him down with thunderbolts) is based on the *Thebaid*, a late Roman epic (by Statius) treating a war waged by seven Greek heroes against the city of Thebes. Although Capaneus's arrogant defiance of the gods is a running theme in the *Thebaid*, Statius's description of the warrior's courage in the scenes leading up to his death also reveals elements of nobility. For instance, Capaneus refuses to follow his comrades in a deceitful military operation against the Theban forces under the cover of darkness, insisting instead on fighting fair and square out in the open (*Thebaid* 10.257–59, 482–86). Capaneus's boundless contempt leads to his demise, however, when he climbs atop the walls protecting the city and directly challenges the gods: "Let me feel the force of all your lightning, Jupiter! Or is your thunder only strong enough to frighten little girls and burn the towers of Cadmus, whom you made your son-in-law?" (*Thebaid* 10.904–6). Recalling similar arrogance displayed by the Giants at Phlegra (and their subsequent defeat), the deity gathers his terrifying weapons and strikes Capaneus with a thunderbolt. His hair and helmet aflame, the hero feels the fatal fire burning within and falls from the walls. He finally lies outstretched on the ground below, his lifeless body as immense as that of a Giant. This is the image inspiring Dante's depiction of Capaneus in the defeated pose of the blasphemers, flat on their backs (*Inf.* 14.22).

BRUNETTO LATINI (15) :: One of the most important figures in Dante's life and in the *Divine Comedy*, Brunetto Latini is featured among the sodomites in one of the central cantos of the *Inferno*. Although the poet imagines Brunetto in Hell, Dante the character and Brunetto show great affection and respect for one another during their encounter. Brunetto (ca. 1220–94) was a prominent Guelph who spent many years living in exile in Spain and France, where he composed his encyclopedic work, *Trésor* ("Treasure"; *Inf.* 15.119–20), before returning to Florence in 1266 and assuming positions of great responsibility in the commune and region (notary, scribe, consul, prior). Such was Brunetto's reputation that Giovanni Villani, an early-fourteenth-century chronicler, praised him as the "initiator and master in refining the Florentines" (*Chronicle* 9.10). While Brunetto's own writings, in terms of quality and significance, are far inferior to Dante's, he was perhaps the most influential promoter in the Middle Ages of the essential idea (derived from the Roman writer Cicero) that eloquence, in both oral and written forms, is beneficial to society only when combined with wisdom.

We learn from this episode that Brunetto played a major (if informal) part in Dante's education, most likely as a mentor through his example of using erudition and intelligence in the service of the city. Apart from the reputed frequency of sexual relations among males in this time and place, there is no independent documentation to explain Brunetto's appearance in Dante's poem among the sodomites. We know only that Brunetto was married with three or four children. Many modern scholarly discussions of Dante's Brunetto either posit a substitute vice for the sexual one (linguistic perversion, unnatural political affiliations, a quasi-Manichean heresy) or emphasize some symbolic form of sodomy over the literal act, such as rhetorical perversion, a failed theory of knowledge, or a protohumanist pursuit of immortality.

Brunetto singles out three individuals from the sodomitic group of clerics and famous intellectuals to which he belongs (*Inf.* 15.106–14). **Priscian** (flourished ca. 500 CE), author of an influential textbook on Latin grammar (*Institutiones grammaticae*), is most likely included on the basis of his profession: teachers in the Middle Ages (grammar teachers in particular) "often seem tainted with this vice," as one early commentator puts it, "perhaps because of their access to the boys whom they teach" (Anonimo Fiorentino). **Francesco d'Accorso** (1225–93), son of a famous legal scholar (Accursius), was himself a distinguished law professor at the University of Bologna; in 1273, much to the chagrin of the Bolognese (who confiscated his property), he traveled to England with King Edward I (who passed through Italy on his return from the Middle East), where he took a teaching position at Oxford and assisted the king in reforming the laws. Pope Boniface VIII ("Servant of Servants"; *Inf.* 15.112), had **Andrea de' Mozzi**, the bishop of Florence, transferred to Vicenza (in Veneto) in 1295 because of his alleged depravity and stupidity: Brunetto's reference to Andrea's "mal protesi nervi" ("wickedly taut tendons"; *Inf.* 15.114) strongly suggests sexual activity (*nervus* often denotes "penis" in Latin literature), and early commentators mock the bishop's intelligence by recounting examples from his sermons, such as his saying that "God's grace is like goat turds, which drop from above and fall scattered in many places" (Benvenuto), and his comparison of divine providence to a mouse, who from his hole sees others without being seen himself (Serravale).

THREE FLORENTINE SODOMITES (16) :: In circle three CIACCO informed Dante that Tegghiaio and Iacopo Rusticucci were among the Florentine leaders bent on doing good whose souls nonetheless inhabit Lower Hell (*Inf.* 6.79–87). Dante now finds them, together with Guido Guerra, punished by a rain of infernal fire for their sodomitic behavior. Virgil commands Dante to treat these three men, despite their wretched state, with great respect (*Inf.* 16.13–18). As they turn together in a circle, moving like wrestlers (naked and oiled) preparing to strike, the three Florentine sodomites are introduced. **Guido Guerra**, grandson of the "good Gualdrada" (*Inf.* 16.37) and Count Guido the Elder (an illustrious Tuscan family), was a Guelph who played a leading role in defeating the Ghibellines at Benevento in 1266. Like Guido, **Tegghiaio Aldobrandi** (a nobleman from the powerful Adimari family) had advised the Florentine Guelphs against marching on Siena, counsel that should have been heeded (*Inf.* 16.41–42) since this expedition resulted in the Ghibelline victory at Montaperti in 1260 (Circle 6, "Guelphs and Ghibellines"). The speaker, **Iacopo Rusticucci**, was a Guelph neighbor and colleague of Tegghiaio from a lower social class. Iacopo's claim to have been harmed most by his "fierce wife" (*Inf.* 16.45) is taken by most early commentators to mean that she was the catalyst for his sexual relations with other men, though Pietro (one of Dante's sons) tells a story involving both male-male relations and "unnatural" sexual acts with his wife: once after Iacopo had brought a boy up to his room, his wife, wishing to defame him, opened the window and shouted, "Fire! Fire!" Iacopo rushed out of the room and threatened to beat his wife, who promptly yelled to the approaching neighbors not to bother, the fire had been put out; because of this, Pietro concludes, Iacopo may have forced her to engage in activities "different from those which nature decrees."

Little is known about **Guglielmo Borsiere**, a sodomite who, according to Iacopo, has arrived only recently and can therefore attest to the current (sorry) state of Florentine society (*Inf.* 16.64–72). Borsiere's name (*borsa* means "purse") suggests that he may have been a purse maker. One early commentator believes he was a good and generous man who, out of dislike for his business, began to spend his time at the courts and homes of noblemen (Benvenuto); Boccaccio wrote a novella in which Borsiere, a worthy and eloquent man of court, shames a miser into changing his ways (*Decameron* 1.8).

USURERS (17) :: Dante observes a group of usurers seated on the hot ground of the seventh circle's innermost ring. Hanging from the neck of each shade is a colorful purse displaying the emblem of the family to which he belonged (*Inf.* 17.55–57). The first purse Dante sees, yellow with a blue lion (*Inf.* 17.58–60), identifies its wearer as a member of the **Gianfigliazzi** family of Florence, most likely Catello di Rosso, who, together with his brother, practiced usury in France before returning to Florence and leaving his family in financial ruin following his death in 1283. The figure of a white goose against a bloodred background (*Inf.* 17.61–63) marks the wearer of this purse as an **Obriachi**, another Florentine family of usurers; in 1298 a certain Locco Obriachi loaned money in Sicily. The usurer who rudely addresses Dante (telling him to beat it) and concludes the visit with a lewd gesture (*Inf.* 17.64–75) identifies himself as a Paduan, his purse bearing the emblem (a fat blue cow against a white background) of the powerful **Scrovegni** family; while many family members were known as usurers, in Dante's day a certain Reginaldo (whose son Arrico financed the Scrovegni chapel, made famous by Giotto's frescoes) was legendary for his greed. The Paduan speaker foretells the arrival of two usurers still alive at the time of

Dante's journey: his compatriot, Vitaliano (*Inf.* 17.67–69), identified by most early commentators as **Vitaliano del Dente**, a moneylender who became *podestà* of Padua (head of the commune) in 1307; and **Giovanni Buiamonte** ("the sovereign knight who will bring the bag with three goats"; *Inf.* 17.72–73), a member of the Becchi family, which, through its financial business, became one of the wealthiest in Florence (though Giovanni went bankrupt and died in wretched poverty).

GERYON (16–17) :: Geryon, a cruel king slain by Hercules, who is merely mentioned in Virgil's *Aeneid* as having a "three-bodied" form (6.289, 8.202), stands out as one of Dante's most complex creatures. With an honest face, a colorful and intricately patterned reptilian hide, hairy paws, and a scorpion's tail, Geryon is an image of fraud (*Inf.* 17.7–27), the realm to which he transports Dante and Virgil (circle eight). Strange as he is, Geryon offers some of the best evidence of Dante's attention to realism. The poet compares Geryon's upward flight to the precise movements of a diver swimming to the surface of the sea (*Inf.* 16.130–36), and he helps us imagine Geryon's descent by noting the sensation of wind rising from below and striking the face of a traveler in flight (*Inf.* 17.115–17). By comparing Geryon to a sullen, resentful falcon (*Inf.* 17.127–36), Dante also adds a touch of psychological realism to the episode: Geryon may in fact be bitter because he was tricked into helping the travelers; Virgil had used Dante's knotted belt to lure the monster (*Inf.* 16.106–23). Dante had used this belt, he informs us long after the fact (*Inf.* 16.106–8), to try to capture the colorfully patterned LEOPARD that impeded his ascent of the mountain in *Inferno* 1.31–36 (Dark Wood, "Three Beasts").

Suggestively associated with the sort of factual truth so wondrous that it appears to be false (*Inf.* 16.124), Geryon is thought by some readers to represent the poem itself or perhaps a negative double of the poem.

Allusions

VIOLENCE :: Virgil explains to Dante that sins of violence are categorized according to the victim: other people (one's neighbor), oneself, or God (*Inf.* 11.28–33). Those who perpetrate violence against other people or their property (murderers and bandits) are punished in the first ring of the seventh circle, a river of blood (*Inferno* 12). Those who do violence against themselves or their own property—suicides and squanderers (more self-destructive than the prodigal in circle four)—inhabit the second ring, a horrid forest (*Inferno* 13). The third ring, enclosed by the first two, is a barren plain of sand ignited by flakes of fire. These torment three separate groups of violent offenders against God: those who offend God directly (blasphemers; *Inferno* 14); those who violate nature, God's offspring (sodomites; *Inferno* 15–16); and those who harm industry and the economy, offspring of nature and therefore grandchild of God (usurers; *Inferno* 17). Associating the sins of these last two groups with Sodom and Cahors (*Inf.* 11.49–50), Dante draws on the biblical destruction of Sodom (and Gomorrah) by fire and brimstone (Genesis 19:24–25) and medieval depictions of citizens of Cahors (a city in southern France) as usurers. Dante's emotional reactions to the shades in the seventh circle range from neutral observation of the murderers and compassion for a suicide to respect for several Florentine sodomites and revulsion at the sight and behavior of the lewd usurers.

Although writers of classical Rome admired by Dante allowed—and at times praised—**suicide** as a response to political defeat or personal disgrace, his Christian tradition emphatically condemned suicide as a sin without exception. Thomas Aquinas, for instance, warned that suicide violates the natural law of self-preservation, harms the community at large, and usurps God's disposition of life and death (*Summa theologiae* 2.2.64.5). Dante's attitude toward Pier della Vigna in *Inferno* 13 and his placement of famous suicides in other locations (DIDO, for example [Circle 2, "Famous Lovers"]) may suggest a more nuanced view.

Dante's inclusion of **sodomy**, understood here as sexual relations between males but not necessarily homosexuality in terms of sexual orientation, is consistent with strong theological and legal declarations in the Middle Ages condemning such activities as contrary to nature. Penalties could include confiscation of property and even capital punishment. In Dante's day, male-male relations, often between a mature man and an adolescent, were common in Florence despite these denunciations.

Usury was similarly condemned, particularly after it was equated with heresy (and therefore made punishable by the Inquisition) at the Council of Vienne in 1311. Based on biblical passages—the pronouncement that fallen man must earn his bread "with labour and toil" (Genesis 3:17), Jesus's appeal to his followers to "lend, hoping for nothing thereby" (Luke 6:35)—medieval theologians considered the lending of money at interest to be sinful. Thomas Aquinas, in his commentary on Aristotle's *Politics*, asserted that usury, like sodomy, is contrary to nature because "it is in accordance with nature that money should increase from natural goods and not from money itself" (1.8.134). Forese Donati, a Florentine friend of Dante who appears in *Purgatorio* 23–24, insinuated, in an exchange of insulting sonnets with the poet, that Dante's father was himself a usurer or money changer.

PHLEGETHON (12, 15) :: Literally a "river of fire" (Virgil, *Aeneid* 6.550–51), Phlegethon is the name Dante gives to the river of hot blood that fills the first ring of circle seven. Those who have committed violent offenses against others—spillers of blood themselves—are submerged in the river to a level corresponding to their guilt. Dante does not identify the river (described in detail in *Inferno* 12.46–54 and 12.100–139) until the travelers have crossed it (Dante on the back of Nessus) and passed through the forest of the suicides. They then approach a red stream flowing out from the inner circumference of the forest across the plain of sand (*Inf.* 14.76–84). Even after Virgil explains the common source of all the rivers in Hell, Dante fails to realize, without further explanation, that the red stream in fact connects to the river of blood he had previously crossed, here identified as the Phlegethon (*Inf.* 14.121–35).

POLYDORUS (13) :: If Dante had believed what he read in the *Aeneid*, Virgil would not have had to make him snap one of the branches to know that the suicide-shades and the trees are one and the same—this, at least, is what Virgil says to the wounded suicide-tree (*Inf.* 13.46–51). Virgil here alludes to the episode of the "bleeding bush" from his *Aeneid* (3.22–68). The "bush" in that case was Polydorus, a young Trojan prince who was sent by his father (Priam, king of Troy) to the neighboring Kingdom of Thrace when Troy was besieged by the Greeks. After

Polydorus arrived bearing a large amount of gold, King Polymnestor, to whom the youth's welfare had been entrusted, murdered the young Trojan and took possession of his riches. Aeneas unwittingly discovers Polydorus's unburied corpse when he uproots three leafy branches to serve as cover for a sacrificial altar: the Trojan hero twice freezes with terror when dark blood drips from the uprooted branches; the third time, a voice, rising from the ground, begs Aeneas to stop causing harm and identifies itself as Polydorus. The plant-man explains how the flurry of spears that pierced his body eventually took the form of the branches Aeneas now plucks. The Trojans honor Polydorus with a proper burial before leaving the accursed land.

OLD MAN OF CRETE (14) :: Dante invents the story of the large statue of an old man, located in Mount Ida on the island of Crete, for both practical and symbolic purposes (*Inf.* 14.94–120). Constructed of a descending hierarchy of materials—gold head, silver arms and chest, brass midsection, iron for the rest (except for one clay foot)—the statue recalls the various ages of humankind (from the golden age to the iron age; Ovid, *Metamorphoses* 1.89–150) in a pessimistic view of history and civilization devolving from best to worst. Dante's statue also resembles the statue that appears in King Nebuchadnezzar's dream in the Bible; the meaning of this dream is revealed in a vision to Daniel, who informs the king that the composition of the statue signifies a declining succession of kingdoms all inferior to the eternal Kingdom of God (Daniel 2:31–45). That the statue is off-balance, leaning more heavily on the clay foot and facing Rome ("as if in a mirror"), probably reflects Dante's conviction that society was suffering due to the excessive political power of the pope and the absence of a strong secular ruler.

Although the statue is not itself found in Hell, the tears that flow down the crack in its body (only the golden head is whole) represent all the suffering of humanity and thus become the river in Hell that goes by different names according to region: Acheron, Styx, Phlegethon, Cocytus (*Inf.* 14.112–20).

PHAETHON AND ICARUS (17) :: As he descends aboard Geryon through the infernal atmosphere, Dante recalls the classical stories of previous aviators (*Inf.* 17.106–14). Phaethon, attempting to confirm his genealogy as the son of Apollo, bearer of the sun, took the reins of the sun-chariot against his father's advice. Unable to control the horses, Phaethon scorched a large swath of the heavens; with the earth's fate hanging in the balance, Jove killed the boy with a thunderbolt (Ovid, *Metamorphoses* 1.750–79, 2.1–339). DAEDALUS (see "Minotaur" above), seeking to escape from the island of Crete, made wings for himself and his son by binding feathers with thread and wax. Icarus, ignoring his father's warnings, flew too close to the sun; the wax melted and the boy crashed into the sea (*Metamorphoses* 8.183–235). Daedalus was so heartbroken that he was unable to depict Icarus's fall in his carvings on the gates of a temple he built to honor Apollo (Virgil, *Aeneid* 6.14–33).

Experiencing flight for the first (presumably the only) time in his life—aboard a "filthy image of fraud" (*Inf.* 17.7), no less—Dante understandably identifies with these two figures whose reckless flying led to their tragic deaths.

Significant Verses

Io vidi gente sotto infino al ciglio (*Inf.* 12.103)
I saw people submerged up to their brow

Uomini fummo, e or siam fatti sterpi (*Inf.* 13.37)
We once were men and are now made into stumps

ingiusto fece me contra me giusto (*Inf.* 13.72)
it made me unjust against my just self

gridò: "Qual io fui vivo, tal son morto" (*Inf.* 14.51)
[He] shouted: "As I was in life, so I am in death"

rispuosi: "Siete voi qui, ser Brunetto?" (*Inf.* 15.30)
I replied: "Is that you here, Ser Brunetto?"

m'insegnavate come l'uom s'etterna (*Inf.* 15.85)
you taught me how man makes himself eternal

La faccia sua era faccia d'uom giusto (*Inf.* 17.10)
His face was the face of a just man

Study Questions

1 :: Why does this region contain so many hybrid creatures?

2 :: In the opening description of the forest (*Inf.* 13.1–9), note how Dante's use of anaphora, the repetition of words at the beginning of successive lines (more evident in the Italian) reinforces his conception of suicide. Look at the language and imagery of this and other passages in *Inferno* 13: how do they contribute to Dante's conception of suicide and the suicidal state of mind?

3 :: Look for ways in which Dante might be said to participate in this idea of suicide. Consider his situation in the dark wood (*Inferno* 1–2) as well as his behavior here in the forest of the suicides.

4 :: Capaneus's continued defiance of Jove in Hell draws a harsh response from Virgil, who explains to Dante that this unabated rage only adds to the blasphemer's punishment (*Inf.* 14.61–72). What do you think? Could Virgil be wrong and Capaneus actually gain a measure of satisfaction from his continuing contempt? Or does the logic of Hell require only punishment and suffering?

5 :: How does Dante (character and poet) treat the sodomites in *Inferno* 15–16? What are possible implications of this treatment?

6 :: We learn in *Inferno* 16 that Dante once thought to capture the leopard (*Inf.* 1.31–43) with a cord, which he now gives to Virgil to summon Geryon (*Inf.* 16.106–14), the "filthy image of fraud" (*Inf.* 17.7). What connections do you see among Geryon, the cord, and the leopard? How might this new information help us to interpret the THREE BEASTS (Dark Wood) from *Inferno* 1 (leopard, lion, and she-wolf)?

7 :: What does Dante's presentation of the usurers tell us about his attitude toward money and economics?

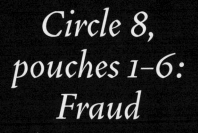

Circle 8, pouches 1–6: Fraud

INFERNO 18–23

CIRCLE EIGHT, also called Malebolge ("evil pouches"), contains ten concentric ditches corresponding to different categories of fraud. The embankments separating the ditches are connected by stone bridges. Dante and Virgil view the shades by walking along the embankments and across the bridges, and at times by descending into a ditch. Punished in the first six ditches are (in order) pimps and seducers, flatterers, simonists (corrupt religious leaders), soothsayers, barrators (crooked public officials), and hypocrites. Jason, leader of the Argonauts, captures Dante's attention among the seducers being whipped by horned demons. In the next ditch, Dante recognizes a flatterer from Lucca wallowing in excrement. After verbally thrashing Pope Nicholas III, stuffed upside down in the ground for prostituting the church, Dante is himself rebuked by Virgil for weeping at the sight of the soothsayers, whose necks are twisted so that tears wet their buttocks. Barrators, immersed in a sea of boiling pitch, are tortured by a band of devils, whose malicious intentions force Virgil to grab Dante and slide down into the sixth pouch. There the travelers find Caiaphas; nailed to the ground, he is trampled by other hypocrites weighed down by gilded, lead-lined cloaks.

Encounters

VENEDICO CACCIANEMICO (18) :: Dante recognizes Venedico Caccianemico, despite the shade's attempt to avoid detection, among the pimps in the first pouch of circle eight (*Inf.* 18.40–66). A Guelph leader from Bologna who served as *podestà* (political head) of several cities between 1264 and 1286 (Imola, Milan, Pistoia), Venedico was reported to have curried favor with the Marquis d'Este (Obizzo II or his son Azzo VIII) by subjecting his own sister, the beautiful Ghisolabella, to the man's sordid desires. Venedico's claim to be joined in this pouch by so many fellow citizens (more than the number of people currently living between Bologna's eastern and western boundaries, the rivers Savena and Reno) reflects the city's reputation for this sort of activity. All the Bolognese, according to one early commentator (Lana), were exceedingly generous with pimping their relatives and friends. Another commentator (Anonimo Fiorentino) attributes the prevalence of this vice to a combustible mixture of greed (on the part of Bolognese men) and the presence of young men coming from many other towns to study at Bologna's celebrated university.

JASON (18) :: Jason, leader of the Argonauts (named for the *Argos*, the first ship) in their quest for the golden fleece of Colchis, stands out in the first ditch among the seducers—who circle the pit in the direction opposite that of the pimps and panderers—as a large, regal figure enduring the torments of Hell with no outward sign of suffering (*Inf.* 18.83–85). Jason earned his place in this ditch through his habit of loving and leaving women: first Hypsipyle of Lemnos, whom Jason seduced and impregnated before abandoning, and then Medea (daughter of the king of Colchis), whose magic enabled Jason to obtain the fleece by yoking fire-breathing oxen to a plow and putting to sleep the dragon guarding the fleece (*Inf.* 18.91–96). Jason later left Medea (whom he had married) to wed Creusa. Medea brutally avenged Jason's disaffection by murdering their two children and poisoning Jason's new wife. Dante's primary sources are Ovid (*Metamorphoses* 7.1–403; *Heroides* 6 and 12) and Statius (*Thebaid* 5.403–98).

ALESSIO INTERMINEI AND THAÏS (18) :: Sunk in excrement at the bottom of the second pouch of circle eight are the flatterers, one of whom Dante recalls having seen alive, with "dry hair," in the world above (*Inf.* 18.118–26): **Alessio Interminei** belonged to a family of prominent white Guelphs from Lucca. He apparently died between December 1295 (when documents show him still alive) and spring of 1300, the time of Dante's journey. One commentator, dramatically elaborating on Dante's presentation, says Alessio "could not speak without seasoning his words with the oil of flattery: he greased and licked everyone, even the cheapest, most vile servants; to put it briefly, he absolutely oozed flattery, he utterly reeked of it" (Benvenuto). The rhyme words in Dante's description of Alessio are ONOMATOPOEIC (Circle 2, "Minos"): the sticking double *c*'s in *Lucca, zucca, stucca* (*Inf.* 18.122, 124, 126) echo the sound made by Alessio as he beats his feces-covered head (*Inf.* 18.124), and indeed by all the flatterers as they slap their bodies, immersed in excrement, with their palms (*Inf.* 18.105). Virgil directs Dante's attention to a second flatterer, a filthy woman with tousled hair who alternately squats and stands while scratching herself with "shit-filled nails" (*Inf.* 18.127–35). This is **Thaïs**, a Greek courtesan who, Virgil says, shamelessly flattered her lover. In the play by Terence (second century BCE) in which Thaïs originally appears (*The Eunuch*), her lover, the soldier Thraso, sends her the gift of a slave through an intermediary, the "parasite" Gnatho; when Thraso asks Gnatho if Thaïs is pleased with the gift, Gnatho flatters Thraso with an exaggerated response. Dante's attribution of the flattery to Thaïs herself is likely due to a misunderstanding caused by an ambiguous passage in Cicero's *On Friendship* (26.98).

POPE NICHOLAS III (19) :: Nicholas is the simonist pope who, because he is stuck headfirst in a hole, mistakenly believes Dante to be **Pope Boniface VIII** (below), somehow present in the third pit several years before his time (*Inf.* 19.52–57). When the confusion is cleared up, Nicholas informs Dante that he foresees the damnation (for simony) not only of Boniface but of **Pope Clement V** as well (below). Born into the powerful Orsini family of Rome, Giovanni Gaetano was appointed head of the Inquisition (1262) before being elected pope and taking the name Nicholas in 1277. Nicholas expanded papal political control by annexing parts of Romagna, as far north as Bologna and Ferrara; he also forged a compromise in the Franciscan movement between the moderates and the radical spiritualists. He was known, on the one hand, for his high moral standards and care for the poor, and on the other for his shameless nepotism (derived from *nipote,* the Italian word for nephew, niece, and grandchild). Nicholas himself states that he was guilty of favoring the "cubs" in his family (Orsini, the family name, translates to "little bears"; *Inf.* 19.70–72): he in fact filled positions for three new cardinals with relatives and appointed other family members to high posts in the papal state. Nicholas died in 1280 and was buried in Saint Peter's in Rome.

SOOTHSAYERS (20) :: After rebuking Dante for pitying the soothsayers, whose heads are twisted so they face backward (*Inf.* 20.19–30), Virgil identifies eight individuals (from the ancient world and Middle Ages) who in one way or another tried to predict (if not to alter) the future. The first two, **Amphiaraus** and **Tiresias**, participated in significant events related to the city of Thebes. Amphiaraus, one of the SEVEN AGAINST THEBES (Circle 7, "Capaneus"), was a prophet from Argos who, seeing evil omens for the war (including his own death), went into seclusion; however, he was forced to fight after his wife Eriphyle wrangled a beautiful necklace from Argia (wife of Polynices, the son of Oedipus and Jocasta). The prophecy was fulfilled when the earth opened and Amphiaraus, together with his horses and chariot, fell down into the underworld (Statius, *Thebaid* 2.299–305, 4.187–213, 7.690–8.126). Tiresias, arguably the most famous soothsayer in classical mythology, was a Theban citizen whose prophetic powers played a prominent role in his city's mythic history, but Dante's passage (*Inf.* 20.40–45) describes one version of the extraordinary circumstances through which he obtained the gift of prophecy in the first place: Tiresias, having been transformed from a man to a woman when he used his staff to strike two copulating snakes, was changed back into a man after he struck the same two snakes again seven years later. He subsequently took Jupiter's side in an argument with Juno over whether men or women derive greater pleasure from lovemaking (Tiresias, based on personal experience, reported that female pleasure is greater); in response, Juno struck him blind, prompting Jupiter to grant him, as compensation, the power of prophecy (Ovid, *Metamorphoses* 3.316–40). The next two soothsayers recognized by Virgil are **Aruns** and **Manto** (*Inf.* 20.46–56). Aruns, a venerable Etruscan seer, conducted an elaborate ritual (including the gruesome examination of a slaughtered bull's entrails) that foretold the horror of civil war between Pompey and Caesar (Lucan, *Pharsalia* 1.584–638). Manto, the daughter of Tiresias, was also capable of foretelling the future (Ovid, *Metamorphoses* 6.157–62); after the fall of Thebes and the death of her father, she journeyed to Italy (see "Mantua" below).

Although Virgil explicitly identifies the next soothsayer in the fourth pouch as a character from his own poem (which he says Dante knows from start to finish; *Inf.* 20.114), his description of **Eurypylus** in *Inferno* 20.106–11 as an augur who (together with Calchas) determined the propitious time for the Greeks to set sail for Troy (from Aulis) differs from the account in *Aeneid* 2.114–19: there Eurypylus is a soldier (not a seer, as Calchas is) sent to Apollo's oracle to learn what the Greeks must do to calm the heavens so they can leave Troy and sail back to Greece. Perhaps Dante assumes that Eurypylus was entrusted with this mission because he was himself a soothsayer. Finally, Virgil points out three figures from the Middle Ages known for their skills in the magical arts (*Inf.* 20.115–20). **Michael Scot** (born ca. 1175 in Scotland) was a brilliant scholar who translated works by ARISTOTLE and AVERROËS (Circle 1) from Arabic into Latin, served as court astrologer to Emperor

FREDERICK II (Circle 6), and wrote treatises on the occult sciences; tales of his magical prowess were widespread (Boccaccio calls him "a great master in necromancy" in *Decameron* 8.9), including the claim (which Benvenuto reports even while questioning its veracity) that Scot accurately predicted he would die from being hit on the head by a small rock. **Guido Bonatti** wrote a popular work on astrology in which he claims to have practiced his "science" on behalf of prominent political leaders (including Frederick II, Guido Novello da Polenta, and Guido da Montefeltro), often in the course of military campaigns; he says the Ghibelline victory at MONTAPERTI (Circle 6, "Guelphs and Ghibellines") was due in part to his astrological calculations. Benvenuto of Parma, nicknamed **Asdente** ("Toothless"), was a shoemaker in the late thirteenth century who appears to have earned great admiration for his many accurate prophecies, including the defeat of Frederick II at Parma in 1248; Dante, calling Asdente the "cobbler of Parma," attests to the soothsayer's notoriety (as distinct from "nobility") in *Convivio* 4.16.6.

MALEBRANCHE (21–22) :: Dante invents the name *Malebranche* ("Evil Claws") for the devils of the fifth ditch who bring to Hell and torment the shades of corrupt political officials and employees (*Inf.* 21.29–42). Similar to the velociraptors of Michael Crichton's *Jurassic Park* (and the film adaptation), these demonic creatures are agile, smart, and fierce. Armed with long hooks, the Malebranche keep the shades under the surface of the black pitch, much as cooks' underlings use sharp implements to push chunks of meat down into cauldrons (*Inf.* 21.55–57). Consistent with the political theme of the episode, it is likely that the names Dante coined for individual demons ("Bad Dog," "Sneering Dragon," "Curly Beard," and so on) are based on actual family names of civic leaders in Florence and surrounding towns. As the narrator says, "with saints in church, with gluttons in the tavern!" (*Inf.* 22.14–15).

Malacoda, the leader of the demons, may not be based on any particular person, but his name ("Evil Tail") strongly suggests that it is he (and not Barbariccia, as several commentators and translators suppose) who sends off his troops by making "a bugle of his ass" (*Inf.* 21.139). Samuel Beckett exploits this resonance between Malacoda's name and his uncouth action in a passage from his poem "Malacoda," published in *Echo's Bones and Other Precipitates* (Paris: Europa Press, 1935) and re-issued in *Poems in English* (New York: Grove Press, 1961). In Beckett's poem Malacoda is the "undertaker's man" who has come to prepare a body for burial; he possesses an "expert awe / that felts his perineum mutes his signal / sighing up through the heavy air" (the perineum is the area between the anus and the genitals).

CIAMPOLO AND OTHER BARRATORS (21–22) :: Dante witnesses one of the Malebranche arriving in the fifth pouch with "one of the elders of Saint Zita" (*Inf.* 21.38), an indication that the barrator in the demon's grasp hails from Lucca, where he served on the city's executive council: Saint Zita (ca. 1208–78), who gained fame for humbly enduring hardships as a servant to a noble family from Lucca, became an object of local worship after her death; after accounts of miracles at her tomb, the bishop of Lucca authorized a cult in 1282 (she was canonized in 1696). The demon's statement that everyone from Lucca practices barratry except for **Bonturo** (*Inf.* 21.41) is highly ironic because Bonturo Dati, who became head of the "popular party" of Lucca in the early fourteenth century (he outlived Dante), was actually the most corrupt of all.

Ciampolo (an Italianized version of Jean-Paul), according to early commentators, is the name of the Navarrese tortured by the Malebranche in the fifth pit (for political corruption) before a clever escape: he promises to summon his peers to the surface but jumps back into the pitch as soon as the Malebranche back off (*Inf.* 22.31–123). Nothing is known of this character beyond what Dante provides in the poem. Navarre was a small kingdom in the south of France (in the Pyrenees), and the "good King Thibault" in whose service Ciampolo took bribes (*Inf.* 22.52–54) was probably Thibault II (king of Navarre from 1255 to 1270).

Before his escape, Ciampolo names two additional barrators in the pitch, both associated with Sardinia (*Inf.* 22.81–90): **Fra Gomita**, a friar who worked for Nino Visconti (judge of Gallura, one of Sardinia's four districts), received praise from his master's captured enemies (*Inf.* 22.83–84) when he accepted bribes to set them free; **Michele Zanche**, according to early commentators, governed Logodoro, another of Sardinia's districts, and likely participated in the struggle between Pisa and

Genoa for control of the island, though nothing is known of his crimes of barratry.

JOVIAL FRIARS: CATALANO AND LODERINGO (23) ::
After Virgil and Dante slide down into the sixth pouch (to escape the Malebranche), they encounter among the slow-moving hypocrites two shades whose curiosity is piqued by Dante's presence because he speaks a Tuscan dialect and, from the movement of his throat, appears to be alive (*Inf.* 23.76–93). **Catalano de' Malavolti** and **Loderingo degli Andalò** were founding members of the Knights of the Militia of the Blessed and Glorious Virgin Mary, a military-religious order formed by Bolognese noblemen in 1261 to protect widows and orphans and to promote peacemaking. Due to the luxurious lifestyle and relaxed attitudes of many members, by the 1280s these religious knights became popularly known as *Frati Gaudenti* ("Jovial Friars"; *Inf.* 23.103). In 1266 Pope Clement IV arranged for Catalano (a Guelph) and Loderingo (a Ghibelline) jointly to assume the role of *podestà* (political chief) in Florence to keep the peace between the two factions. Their ostensible neutrality was, however, revealed to be a hypocritical ruse when they favored the Guelph side (probably at the pope's bidding) by fomenting the popular uprising that led to the banishment of prominent Ghibelline families and, in several cases, the destruction of their houses (located in the area around the "Gardingo," a watchtower; *Inf.* 23.108). Catalano informs Virgil that he and Dante will soon come upon the ruins of the next bridge, which the travelers can climb to extricate themselves from the ditch. Malacoda therefore lied to Virgil when he said this bridge was intact (*Inf.* 21.109–11)—an unsurprising development since, as Catalano says, the devil is the "father of lies" (*Inf.* 23.144).

CAIAPHAS (23) :: Caiaphas is the high priest of Jerusalem who, according to Christian scripture, advised a council of chief priests and Pharisees that it would be expedient for one man to "die for the people" so that "the whole nation perish not" (John 11:50). Considering this proclaimed interest in the welfare of his people to be false and self-serving, Dante places Caiaphas among the hypocrites in the sixth pit, with an added *contrapasso:* because Caiaphas and other members of the council (including Caiaphas's father-in-law, Annas) supposedly called on the Romans to crucify Jesus (John 18:12–40, 19:1–18), they are now themselves crucified on the floor of the pit (*Inf.* 23.109–20). Dante here endorses the repugnant view, widely held by Christians in the Middle Ages, that the crucifixion of Jesus was justification for the persecution of Jews (*Inf.* 23.121–23), including the siege of Jerusalem and the destruction of the Second Temple by the Romans (under Titus) in 70 CE.

Allusions

FRAUD: PIMPING AND SEDUCING (18), FLATTERY (18), SIMONY (19), SOOTHSAYING (20), BARRATRY (21–22), HYPOCRISY (23) :: The offenses punished in circles eight and nine, the two lowest circles of Hell, all fall under the rubric of fraud, a form of malice (as Virgil explains in *Inferno* 11.22–27) unique to human beings and therefore more displeasing to God than sins of CONCUPIS-CENCE (Circles 2–5; see Dark Wood, "Three Beasts") and VIOLENCE (Circle 7). All versions of fraud involve the malicious use of reason; what distinguishes circle eight from circle nine is the perpetrator's relationship to his or her victim: if there exists no bond besides the "natural" one common to all humanity, the guilty soul suffers in one of the ten concentric ditches that constitute circle eight, but those who victimize someone with whom they share a special bond of trust (relatives, fellow citizens or partisans, guests, benefactors) are punished in the lowest circle.

Physically connected by bridges, the ditches of circle eight contain fraudulent shades whose particular vices and actions similarly serve to interconnect the cantos and their themes in this part of the poem. Thus the **pimps and seducers**, whipped by horned demons in the first ditch, relate to the **flatterers**—disgustingly dipped in the excrement of the second ditch—through the sexualized figure of Thaïs, a prostitute from the classical tradition who falsely praises her "lover" (*Inf.* 18.127–35). These first two ditches are presented in a single canto (18). Images of degraded sexuality are even more prominent in the next canto (19). Here Dante presents **simony**, the abuse of power within the church, as a form of spiritual prostitution, fornication, and rape (*Inf.* 19.1–4, 55–57, 106–11), a perversion of the holy matrimony conventionally posited between Christ (groom) and the church (bride). Simon Magus, the man for whom simony is named (*Inf.* 19.1), was himself a magician or sooth-sayer, the profession of those punished in the fourth ditch (*Inferno* 20). Simony and **soothsaying** are further linked through personal declarations by Dante and Virgil aimed at separating truth from falsehood: Dante sets the record straight when he announces that he shattered a marble baptismal basin to prevent someone from drowning in it (*Inf.* 19.19–21), while Virgil is equally emphatic that his native city, Mantua, was named after the prophetess Manto with no recourse to such dubious rituals as casting lots or interpreting signs (*Inf.* 20.91–99). **Barratry**, or political corruption (fifth ditch), the crime with which Dante himself was falsely charged when he was forced into exile, links back to similar abuses within the church (simony) and points ahead to the sin of **hypocrisy**. The longest single episode of the *Inferno*, launched when Virgil confidently believes the promise of the devils guarding the fifth ditch, concludes when the travelers make a narrow escape into the sixth ditch and Virgil learns from a hypocrite that he has been duped (*Inf.* 23.133–48). Dante adorns the hypocrites in religious garb, hooded cloaks similar to the elegant ones worn by the Benedictine monks at Cluny (in France), in accordance with Jesus's condemnation of false piety: just as hypocritical scribes and Pharisees resemble tombs that appear clean and beautiful on the outside while containing bones of the dead (Matthew 23:27–28), so the bright golden cloaks of Dante's hypocrites conceal linings of heavy lead (*Inf.* 23.64–66).

MALEBOLGE (18) :: Malebolge, the name Dante gives to circle eight, translates to "evil pouches" (*male* means "evil" and *bolgia* is a Tuscan dialect word for "purse" or "pouch"). Dante describes its overall structure—ten concentric ravines or ditches, similar to moats (with connecting bridges) around a castle—in *Inferno* 18.1–18, even before the travelers pass through the region. The character Dante likely saw the entire layout as he descended aboard Geryon, who transported him from circle seven to circle eight (*Inf.* 17.115–26).

SIMON MAGUS (19) :: Simon Magus, the original simonist (*Inf.* 19.1), is described in the Bible as a man from Samaria famous for his magical powers (*magus* means "wizard" or "magician"). Recently converted and baptized, Simon is so impressed with the ability of the apostles Peter and John to confer the Holy Spirit through the laying on of hands that he offers them money to obtain this power for himself; Peter angrily denounces Simon for even thinking this gift could be bought (Acts 8:9–24). An apocryphal book, *Acts of Peter*, tells of a magic contest between the apostle and Simon, now the magician of the emperor Nero in Rome. When Simon, with the aid of a demon, proceeds to fly, Peter crosses himself and Simon promptly crashes to the ground.

POPE BONIFACE VIII (19) :: Boniface, for Dante, is personal and public enemy number one. Benedetto Caetani, a talented and ambitious scholar of canon law, rose quickly through the ranks of the church and was elected pope, taking the name Boniface VIII, soon after the abdication of POPE CELESTINE V in 1294 (Periphery of Hell, "Great Refusal"). (There were rumors that Boniface had intimidated Celestine into abdicating so he could become pope himself.) Boniface's pontificate was marked by a consolidation and expansion of church power, based on the view, expressed in his papal bull *Unam sanctam*, that the pope was not only the spiritual head of Christendom but also superior to the emperor in the secular, temporal realm. Dante, by contrast, firmly held that the pope and the emperor should be coequals, with a balance maintained between the pope's spiritual authority and the emperor's secular authority. Boniface's political ambitions directly affected Dante when the pope, under the pretense of peacemaking, sent Charles of Valois, a French prince, to Florence; Charles's intervention allowed the black Guelphs to overthrow the ruling white Guelphs, whose leaders— including Dante, in Rome at the time to argue Florence's case before Boniface—were sentenced to EXILE (Circle 3, "Florentine Politics"). Dante settles his score with Boniface in the *Divine Comedy* by damning the pope even before his death in 1303 (the journey takes place in 1300): in the pit of the simonists, Pope Nicholas III, who (like all the damned) can see the future, but, since he is buried upside down, cannot see Dante and Virgil, mistakenly assumes that Dante is Boniface come before his time (*Inf.* 19.49–63).

POPE CLEMENT V (19) :: Nicholas III, the simonist pope who mistakes Dante for Boniface VIII, foresees the arrival of another simonist known for even "more sordid deeds" (*Inf.* 19.82), one who will stuff

93

Nicholas and Boniface farther down in the hole when he takes his place upside down with his legs and feet in view. This "lawless shepherd" from the west (*Inf.* 19.83) is Bertrand de Got, a French archbishop who in 1305 became Pope Clement V. Bertrand owed his election to King Philip IV of France, much as the biblical Jason became high priest by bribing King Antiochus (*Inf.* 19.85–87; 2 Maccabees 4:7–26). In return for Philip's support, Clement moved the Holy See from Rome to Avignon (in southern France) in 1309, an action so abhorrent to many (Dante among them) that it came to be known as the "Babylonian captivity." The conflict continued, and after 1377, there were in fact sometimes two popes (or a pope and an antipope, according to one's perspective), one in Rome and one in France. The Great Schism ended in 1417 with the definitive return of the papacy to Rome.

DONATION OF CONSTANTINE (19) :: It was believed in the late Middle Ages that Constantine, the first Christian emperor (ca. 280–337), transferred political control of Italy (and other parts of the West) to the church when he moved the capital of the empire from Rome to Byzantium (which was renamed Constantinople) in the East. Legend held that Constantine gave this gift to Pope Sylvester I, whose baptism of the emperor had cured him of leprosy. Dante, who thought the world better served with political power in the hands of the emperor, bitterly blamed this event for the dire consequences of a wealthy papacy (*Inf.* 19.115–17). The document that authorized this transfer of power, popularly called the Donation of Constantine, was proved by Lorenzo Valla in the fifteenth century to be a fake, probably written in the papal court or in France several centuries after Constantine's death.

MANTUA (20) :: After Virgil identifies the prophetess Manto (daughter of Tiresias) in the pit of the soothsayers, he goes to great pains to explain to Dante that his native city (Mantua) was named after her simply because she had lived and died in the place before it was inhabited by other people (*Inf.* 20.52–93). The city's founders, he says, did not draw lots or resort to augury or divination. It may well be that Dante is allowing Virgil, who himself possessed a widespread reputation in the Middle Ages for WIZARDLIKE POWERS (Circle 5, "Erichtho"), an opportunity to distance his city—and, by extension, himself—from just the sort of activity being punished in the fourth ditch. Virgil's association with magic could derive, for instance, from his eighth *Eclogue*, a poem in which a jealous female shepherd tries witchcraft to win back her lover: "Fetch water and around this altar wind soft wool / And burn the sappy vervain and male frankincense, / For by these magical rituals I hope to turn / My sweetheart's sanity; only spells are lacking now" (64–67). In attempting to exonerate himself, however, Virgil may have committed perjury. Although he insists that his version of the founding of Mantua in *Inferno* 20 is the only true version (any other account, he claims, would be a falsehood; *Inf.* 20.97–99), a different version appears in, of all places, the *Aeneid:* in book 10 of his epic, Virgil explicitly attributes both the founding and naming of Mantua to Manto's son Ocnus, a Tuscan warrior who comes to the aid of Aeneas in the Italian wars: "There, too, another chieftain comes who from / his native coasts has mustered squadrons: Ocnus, / the son of prophesying Manto and / the Tuscan river; Mantua, he gave you / walls and his mother's name—o Mantua..." (198–200). While this account by the author of the *Aeneid* does not explicitly contradict the claim by the Virgil of Dante's *Inferno* that Mantua was named without recourse to magic, it is nonetheless an example of the "city's origin told otherwise."

HARROWING OF HELL (21) :: Malacoda indirectly alludes to Christ's HARROWING OF HELL (Circle 1; see also Circle 5, "Fallen Angels," and Circle 7, "Minotaur") when he states that the bridge on which Virgil and Dante are traveling does not span the next ditch (the sixth). This section of the bridge, according to Malacoda, collapsed during the earthquake that shook the underworld "five hours from this hour yesterday, one thousand two hundred and sixty-six years ago" (*Inf.* 21.112–14). Assuming (as Dante does in *Convivio* 4.23.10–11) that Jesus died in his thirty-fourth year, we can now definitively date Dante's journey to Holy Week of 1300: since Jesus died on Friday close to noon (the common medieval interpretation of "sixth hour"; Luke 23:44), it is presently five hours earlier—7 a.m.—on Holy Saturday. Dante therefore spent the night of Maundy Thursday in the dark wood and, after encountering the three beasts and Virgil the following day, approached the gate of Hell as night fell on Good Friday (*Inf.* 2.1–3). Virgil's own recollection of the earthquake triggered by Christ's Harrowing (*Inf.*

4.52–63, 12.34–45) may help explain his questionable judgment in accepting Malacoda's offer of safe passage, with an escort of ten demons, to a point where another bridge is supposedly intact.

Significant Verses

già t'ho veduto coi capelli asciutti (*Inf.* 18.121)
I've seen you before, with dry hair

se' tu già costí ritto, Bonifazio? (*Inf.* 19.53)
are you already standing there, Boniface?

che sú l'avere e qui me misi in borsa (*Inf.* 19.72)
wealth up above, and myself here, I put in a pouch

Qui vive la pietà quand' è ben morta (*Inf.* 20.28)
Here lives pity when it is good and dead

la verità nulla menzogna frodi (*Inf.* 20.99)
let no falsehood cheat the truth

e disse: "Posa, posa, Scarmiglione!" (*Inf.* 21.105)
and he said: "Down, down, Scarmiglione!"

ed elli avea del cul fatto trombetta (*Inf.* 21.139)
and he had made a bugle of his ass

Oh in etterno faticoso manto! (*Inf.* 23.67)
Oh, for eternity, a tiring mantle!

dietro a le poste de le care piante (*Inf.* 23.148)
following the prints of his dear feet

Study Questions

1 :: Use *Inferno* 18.1–18 to draw an image of Malebolge.

2 :: The *contrapasso* for the flatterers (immersed in excrement) seems clear enough. Explain how the punishments are fitting for the simonists (*Inferno* 19) and the soothsayers (*Inferno* 20).

3 :: Why is Dante so upset by the sight of the contorted soothsayers, and why does Virgil rebuke him for this show of compassion (*Inf.* 20.19–30)?

4 :: What are possible implications of Virgil's differing versions of the founding of Mantua in *Aeneid* 10 and *Inferno* 20.52–99?

5 :: Find examples of deception—individuals tricking one another—in *Inferno* 21–23.

6 :: What is the *contrapasso* for the corrupt public officials in the fifth pouch (*Inferno* 21–22) and for the hypocrites in the sixth pouch (*Inferno* 23)?

7 :: How do the events of *Inferno* 21–23, the longest single episode of the *Inferno* and the "comedy" of the *Divine Comedy*, affect the relationship between Dante and Virgil?

Circle 8,
pouches 7–10:
Fraud

INFERNO 24–30

AFTER CLIMBING OUT of the pit of the hypocrites, Dante and Virgil observe the punishment of fraudulent souls in the remaining four ditches of circle eight. In the seventh ditch Dante sees Vanni Fucci, who is reduced to ashes by a snakebite and then just as quickly regains his human appearance, and other thieves, who undergo transformations between human and reptilian forms. In the next ditch, enveloped in tonguelike flames, are authors of devious stratagems, particularly those involving persuasive speech. Here the Greek hero Ulysses, paired with his sidekick Diomedes, recounts his fatal final voyage, and Guido da Montefeltro, an Italian warlord, tells how he was damned for providing Pope Boniface VIII with fraudulent counsel. In the ninth ditch Dante encounters sowers of discord whose shade-bodies are divided by a sword-wielding devil. The arresting figure of Betran de Born, a poet whose severed head continues to speak, exemplifies the law of *contrapasso*, the correspondence between sin and punishment. Falsifiers—alchemists, counterfeiters, impersonators, and liars—are afflicted with various diseases in the tenth and final ditch of circle eight. Virgil scolds Dante for observing a quarrel between Master Adam (a counterfeiter) and Sinon, the Greek whose lie led to the destruction of Troy.

Encounters

VANNI FUCCI (24–25) :: Vanni Fucci, the thief who is incinerated after receiving a snakebite and then regains his human form, like the Phoenix rising from the ashes (*Inf.* 24.97–111), was a black Guelph from Pistoia, a town not far from rival Florence. He grudgingly admits to having stolen holy objects (possibly silver tablets with images of the Virgin Mary and the apostles) from a chapel in the Pistoian cathedral, a confession he certainly did not offer when another man was accused of the crime and very nearly executed before the true culprits were identified. Vanni subsequently gave up an accomplice, who was executed instead. Dante says he knew Vanni as a man "of blood and anger" (*Inf.* 24.129; he in fact committed numerous acts of violence, including murder), qualities on full display in *Inferno* 24 and 25: he first gets back at his interlocutor by announcing future political events personally painful to Dante—namely, the joining of forces of exiled black Guelphs from Pistoia and Florence to overthrow and banish the white Guelphs of Florence in 1301 (*Inf.* 24.142–51); immediately after this symbolic "screw you!" to Dante, the thief actually gives God the proverbial finger (he makes "figs"—signifying copulation—by placing his thumb between the forefinger and middle finger of each hand) (*Inf.* 25.1–3). Vanni Fucci thus takes the prize as the shade showing the most extreme arrogance toward God in Dante's experience of Hell (*Inf.* 25.13–15).

CACUS (25) :: Cacus is the angry Centaur who seeks to punish Vanni Fucci in the pit of the thieves. Dante presents this horse-man as an elaborate monster, with snakes covering his equine back and a dragon—shooting fire at anyone in the way—astride his human shoulders (*Inf.* 25.16–24). Virgil explains that Cacus is not with the other CENTAURS (Circle 7) patrolling the river of blood in the circle of violence (*Inferno* 12) because he fraudulently stole from a herd of cattle belonging to Hercules, who brutally clubbed Cacus to death (*Inf.* 25.28–33). Virgil portrays Cacus in the *Aeneid* as a half-human, fire-breathing monster inhabiting a cavern under the Aventine hill (near the future site of Rome) filled with gore and the corpses of his victims. Cacus steals Hercules' cattle (four bulls and four heifers) by dragging them backward into his cavern (to conceal evidence of his crime). When Hercules hears the cries of one of his stolen cows, he tears the top off the hill and, to the delight of the native population, strangles Cacus to death (*Aeneid* 8.193–267). The account of Hercules using his massive club to kill Cacus (instead of strangling him) appears in Livy's *Roman History* (1.7.7) and Ovid's *Fasti* (1.575–78).

OTHER THIEVES (25) :: After Dante and Virgil have observed Cacus below in the pouch of the thieves, there appear three new souls in human form (*Inf.* 25.34–39) and two in the guise of reptiles, whose identities will not be known until elaborate transformations have taken place. One of the three men, **Agnel** (*Inf.* 25.68), is attacked by **Cianfa** (*Inf.* 25.43) in the form of a six-footed serpent, and the two fuse into a hideous hybrid creature that is "neither two nor one" (*Inf.* 25.69). Agnel is thought to be Agnello dei Brunelleschi (a member of a prominent Florentine Ghibelline family), who, after the Guelphs came to power, joined the white Guelphs but later switched to the black faction; one commentator (Anonimo Selmiano) claims Agnello took to stealing at a young age, beginning with his parents' purses and progressing to the strongbox at the family business. The same commentator says that Cianfa, thought to belong to the powerful Donati family of Florence, had a reputation for stealing livestock and breaking into shops to empty their safes.

A second man is bitten in the belly by a lizard and the two exchange features (through the medium of smoke that issues from the lizard's mouth and the man's wound)—the man becomes a lizard and the lizard becomes a man. This new man identifies the new lizard (former man) as **Buoso** (*Inf.* 25.140), most likely another member of the Donati family. Buoso, in one version of events (Anonimo Fiorentino, commenting on *Inf.* 25.85–87), stole while he served in public office; when his term expired, Buoso arranged for **Francesco de' Cavalcanti**, the speaker with whom he just exchanged forms, to take over and steal on his behalf. Dante recognizes the new man (former lizard) as Francesco, also known as "Guercio" ("Cross-Eyed"), one who brought grief to Gaville (*Inf.* 25.151) after he was murdered by men from the village (located in the upper valley of the Arno) and his family avenged his death by killing many of the town's inhabitants.

Dante tells us that the only one of the original three men not transformed in any way was **Puccio Sciancato** (*Inf.* 25.145–50), a member of the Florentine Galigai family (his nickname "sciancato" means "lame"). Puccio, a Ghibelline who was banished with his children in 1268 and joined in the peace pact of 1280 with the Guelphs, was renowned for the elegant manner of his heists, which were said to take place in broad daylight.

ULYSSES AND DIOMEDES (26) :: Appearing in a single yet divided flame in the eighth pit of circle eight are Ulysses and Diomedes, two Greek heroes from the war against Troy whose joint punishment reflects their many combined exploits. Because the *Iliad* (recounting the Trojan War) and the *Odyssey* (telling of Ulysses' ten-year wandering before returning home to Ithaca) were not available to Dante, he would have known of these exploits not from Homer's poetry but from parts and reworkings of the Homeric story contained in classical and medieval Latin and vernacular works. Virgil, who writes extensively of Ulysses from the perspective of the Trojan Aeneas (*Aeneid* 2), now as

Dante's guide lists three offenses committed by Ulysses and Diomedes: devising and executing the stratagem of the wooden horse (an ostensible gift that, filled with Greek soldiers, occasioned the destruction of Troy); luring Achilles—hidden by his mother, Thetis, on the island of Skyros—into the war effort (for which Achilles abandoned Deidamia and their son); and stealing the Palladium (a statue of Athena that protected the city of Troy) with the help of a Trojan traitor, Antenora (*Inf.* 26.58–63).

That Virgil is the one to address Ulysses, the "greater horn" of the forked flame (*Inf.* 26.85), is itself noteworthy. On the one hand, this may simply reflect a cultural affinity between Virgil and Ulysses, two men (in Dante's view) from the ancient world. On the other hand, Virgil's appeal to Ulysses, asking the shade to pause and tell his story if the poet was "deserving" based on his "noble verses," rings false (Virgil in fact has nothing good to say about the Greek hero in the *Aeneid*)—so false that some think Virgil may be trying to trick Ulysses by impersonating Homer!

Blissfully ignorant of the *Odyssey*—and either ignorant or dismissive of a medieval account in which Ulysses is killed by Telegonus, son of the enchantress Circe—Dante invents an original version of the final chapter of Ulysses' life, a voyage beyond the boundaries of the known world that ends in shipwreck and death. The voyage itself may or may not be implicated in Ulysses' damnation. Certainly, Ulysses' quest for "virtue and knowledge" (*Inf.* 26.120) embodies a noble sentiment, one consistent with Cicero's praise of Ulysses as a model for the love of wisdom (*On Moral Ends* 5.18.49). Conversely, Ulysses' renunciation of family obligations (*Inf.* 26.94–99) and his effective use of eloquence to win the minds of his men (*Inf.* 26.112–20) may be signs that this voyage is morally unacceptable no matter how noble its goals. You be the judge.

Ulysses, in any case, represents an immensely gifted individual not afraid to exceed established limits and chart new ground. It is perhaps appropriate that Dante prefaces the presentation of Ulysses with a self-directed warning not to abuse his own talent (*Inf.* 26.19–24).

GUIDO DA MONTEFELTRO (27) :: Whereas Virgil addresses the Greek hero Ulysses in *Inferno* 26, Dante himself speaks to Guido da

Montefeltro (a figure from Dante's medieval Italian world) in *Inferno* 27. Guido (ca. 1220–98), a fraudulent character who may himself be a victim of fraud, immediately reveals the limits of his scheming mind when he expresses a willingness to identify himself only because he believes (or claims to believe) that no one ever returns from Hell alive (*Inf.* 27.61–66). T. S. Eliot uses these lines in the Italian original as the epigraph to his famous poem about a modern-day Guido, "The Love Song of J. Alfred Prufrock." Note how the double s's, another outstanding example of ONOMATOPOEIA (Circle 2, "Minos"; see also Circle 8, pouch 2, "Alessio Interminei"), imitate the hissing sound of the speaking flame:

> S'i' credesse che mia risposta fosse
> a persona che mai tornasse al mondo,
> questa fiamma staria sanza piú scosse;
> ma però che già mai di questo fondo
> non tornò vivo alcun, s'i' odo il vero,
> sanza tema d'infamia ti rispondo. (*Inf.* 27.61–66)

> *If I thought my answer was to someone who might return to the*
> *world, this flame would move no more; but since from this depth*
> *it never happened that anyone alive returned (if I hear right),*
> *without fear of infamy I'll answer you.*

Similar to Ulysses, Guido was a sly military-political leader, more fox than lion, who knew "all the tricks and covert ways" of the world (*Inf.* 27.73–78). He was a prominent Ghibelline who led several important military campaigns in central Italy. In the 1270s and the early 1280s he scored decisive victories over Guelph and papal forces before being driven out of Forlì in 1283 (see "Romagna" below). Excommunicated, he later captained the forces of the Pisan Ghibellines against Florence (1288–92); in 1296 POPE BONIFACE VIII (Circle 8, pouch 3) rescinded the excommunication as part of a political strategy to remove the dangerous Guido from the scene. Thus Dante relates how Guido, unlike Ulysses, made an attempt—at least superficially—to change his devious ways when he retired from his active warrior life to become a Franciscan friar (*Inf.* 27.67–68, 79–84). In an earlier work, Dante praises Guido's apparent conversion as a model for how the virtuous individual should retire from worldly affairs late in life (*Convivio* 4.28.8); Dante uses Guido's story for a very different purpose here in the *Inferno*. Now the poet calls into question Guido's pretense to a pious life at the same time that he strikes another blow against the pope he loves to hate: Boniface induces Guido to provide advice for destroying the pope's enemies (he advises Boniface to make and then break a promise of amnesty for the Colonna family) in exchange for the impossible absolution of this sin even before Guido commits it (*Inf.* 27.85–111). It is believed that Guido died (and was buried) in the Franciscan monastery at Assisi in 1298.

MOHAMMED AND ALI (28) :: Consistent with medieval Christian thinking, in which the Muslim world was viewed as a hostile usurper, Dante depicts both Mohammed, the founder of Islam, and his son-in-law Ali as sowers of religious divisiveness. One popular view held that Mohammed had himself been a cardinal who, his papal ambitions thwarted, caused a great schism within Christianity when he and his followers splintered off to form a new religious community. Dante creates a vicious composite portrait of the two holy men, with Mohammed's body split from groin to chin and Ali's face cleft from top to bottom (*Inf.* 28.22–33).

According to tradition, the prophet Mohammed founded Islam in the early seventh century CE at Mecca. Ali married Mohammed's daughter, Fatima, but a dispute over Ali's succession to the caliphate led, after his assassination in 661, to a division among Muslims into Sunni and Shi'ite. Still very much part of the collective memory in Dante's world were the crusades of the twelfth and early thirteenth centuries, in which Christian armies from Europe fought, mostly unsuccessfully and with heavy losses on all sides, to drive Muslims out of the Holy Land. In the Middle Ages, Islam had great influence in Europe in terms of both culture—particularly in medicine, philosophy, and mathematics—and politics: Spain (Al-Andalus) was under complete or partial Muslim control from the eighth through fifteenth centuries.

BERTRAN DE BORN (28) :: Dante selects a troubadour poet, Bertran de Born, for the defining example of *contrapasso*, the logical relationship between the sin and its punishment in Hell (*Inf.* 28.139–42). Because he allegedly instigated a rift between King Henry II of England and his son, the young prince Henry, Bertran is now himself physically divided and demonstrates an infernal version of wireless communication: he carries his decapitated head, which—though separated from the body—inexplicably manages to speak (*Inf.* 28.118–26).

Bertran (ca. 1140–ca. 1215) was a nobleman from a region—primarily in what is now southern France—famous for the production of Provençal literature, most importantly the first lyric poems written in a vernacular romance language. Most of these poems speak of love, but others deal with moral or political themes. In the case of Bertran, Dante likely had in mind the following verses, in which the troubadour celebrates the mayhem and violence of warfare:

> Maces, swords, helmets—colorfully—
> Shields, slicing and smashing,
> We'll see at the start of the melee
> With all those vassals clashing,
> And horses running free
> From their masters, hit, downtread.
> Once the charge has been led,
> Every man of nobility
> Will hack at arms and heads.
> Better than taken prisoner: be dead.
> (Wilhelm, *Lyrics of the Middle Ages*, 91)

Bertran's divisive role, he tells Dante, compares with that of **Achitofel**, a biblical figure who aided Absalom's conspiracy against his father, King David (*Inf.* 28.136–38). Achitofel, who had been David's counselor and whose advice was considered godly, instructed Absalom to sleep with David's concubines (and thereby disgrace his father) and sought permission to raise an army and attack David immediately. However, Absalom, tricked by an infiltrator loyal to David, rejected this last piece of advice and was eventually defeated. Upon the refusal of his counsel, Achitofel returned home and hanged himself (2 Kings 15–17).

OTHER SOWERS OF DISCORD (28–29) :: The other sowers of discord encountered in the ninth pouch span the geopolitical spectrum most important to Dante, from the Roman Empire and Italian regions to the city of Florence and Dante's own extended family. **Pier da Medicina**, whose throat is slit and nose and one ear have been cut off (*Inf.* 28.64–69), claims to have met Dante in the world above, probably somewhere in the vast Po River valley, which extends through the regions of Romagna and Lombardy (*Inf.* 28.70–75). Pier is reported to have poisoned relations between the leading families of Ravenna (Polenta) and Rimini (Malatesta) by falsely informing each side of the malicious intentions of the other. Such scandalmongering explains why he can foresee the murderous actions of Malatestino of Rimini, "that traitor who sees with only one eye" (*Inf.* 28.85): after inviting Guido del Cassero and Angiolello da Carignano, the leading men from Fano, to a meeting at La Cattolica (between Fano and Rimini on the Adriatic coast), Malatestino will have them thrown off their boat and drowned in the sea off the promontory of Focara (*Inf.* 28.76–90). Pier introduces Dante to one who wishes he had never seen Rimini (*Inf.* 28.86–87), a shade who cannot speak because his tongue has been cut out (*Inf.* 28.94–102): this is **Curio** (Gaius Scribonius Curio), who, having fled from Rome after the Senate declared Julius Caesar an enemy, spoke momentous words near Rimini when he urged Caesar not to delay in crossing the Rubicon (a stream separating Cisalpine Gaul from Italy) in 49 BCE (Lucan, *Pharsalia* 1.261–81). This crossing triggered the civil war that left Caesar ruler of Rome and the lands under its control.

Another shade whose hands have been hacked off (blood drips on his face from his raised arms) identifies himself as **Mosca**, a purveyor of words so divisive that they were an "evil seed" for the people of Tuscany (*Inf.* 28.103–8), the city of Florence in particular. Mosca de' Lamberti, whose presence in Lower Hell was previewed by CIACCO (Circle 3), instigated the violent act that passed into history as the origin of the bloody conflict in Florence between GUELPHS AND GHIBELLINES (Circle 6): after Buondelmonte de' Buondelmonti jilted a young woman from the Amidei family and married a woman from the Donati family instead, Mosca told the outraged Amidei clan "a thing done has an end" (*Inf.* 28.107), meaning they should avenge the offense in the harshest manner. Acting on this advice, Lambertuccio degli Amidei and several cohorts (including Mosca) attacked Buondelmonte and stabbed him to death near the statue of Mars at the head of the bridge in Florence (later named the Ponte Vecchio) on Easter Sunday, 1215 (in other versions, 1216). This murder ignited a feud between supporters of the Buondelmonti and the Uberti (one of whom participated in the attack) that escalated into the bitter rivalry of Florentine Guelphs and Ghibellines (headed by the Buondelmonti and Uberti respectively; Villani, *Chronicle* 6.38).

Dante's own family apparently was not immune to the codes of honor implicated in the divisive violence punished in Hell. Although Dante did not see the relative he expected to find before the travelers moved away from the ninth ditch, Virgil heard the man called by his name and observed him pointing to Dante with a threatening gesture (*Inf.* 29.16–30). **Geri del Bello**, a first cousin of Dante's father, is accused by several early commentators of being a falsifier—specifically, a counterfeiter (Lana), an alchemist (Anonimo Fiorentino), and an imposter (Lana, Buti)—as well as a sower of discord; he may therefore serve as a bridge between the final two pouches of circle eight. Geri, named in documents of 1269 and 1276, is believed to have fueled dissension among members of the Sacchetti family, for which, according to Dante's son Pietro, he was murdered by Brodaio dei Sacchetti. That Geri's murder had not been avenged by Dante or other relatives at the time of the journey (1300) is cause for Geri's anger and Dante's shame (*Inf.* 29.31–36). Such revenge supposedly took place some thirty years after Geri's death when his nephews killed one of the Sacchetti. The blood feud lasted until the two families formally reconciled in 1342.

GRIFFOLINO AND CAPOCCHIO (29) :: Propped up against one another in the tenth and final pit, furiously scratching their itching scabs, are two men punished for falsifying metals (alchemy) in order to deceive others. (It is important to note that alchemical studies aimed at discovering the common source of all metals and transmuting base metals into gold were not always condemned in the Middle Ages and were in fact discussed and conducted by eminent philosophers and theologians, including Albert the Great and Roger Bacon.) The first speaker, identified as **Griffolino d'Arezzo**, explains that he was executed not as a result of his unlawful activity but because of ill-advised joking or bravado: as part of a scheme to fleece a wealthy and gullible friend from Siena (Albero), Griffolino said he could teach him to fly. When Griffolino failed to make good on his promise, Albero complained to a powerful man who was like a father to him; this man, the bishop of Siena (or perhaps the inquisitor), had Griffolino burned at the stake for heresy or the practice of black magic (*Inf.* 29.109–20).

The second alchemist, identifying himself as **Capocchio**, clearly expects Dante to recognize him (*Inf.* 29.133–39). The amusing anecdotes told by early commentators certainly attest to Dante's firsthand knowledge of Capocchio. Benvenuto reports that one time, on Good Friday, Capocchio skillfully painted the entire story of the passion of Christ on his fingernails; when Dante asked what he had done, Capocchio promptly licked the paint off his nails, much to Dante's displeasure. Another commentator claims that Dante and Capocchio had studied together in Florence, and that Capocchio allegedly transformed his talent at mimicking people and objects into an ability to falsify metals (Anonimo Fiorentino). What we do know, based on a document in the Siena state archives (dated August 3, 1292), is that three men were paid to carry out justice by burning Capocchio, presumably for his fraudulent alchemical practices. Picking up on Dante's derisive comment on the foolishness of the Sienese (*Inf.* 29.121–23), Capocchio sarcastically reinforces Dante's judgment by naming four members of the infamous SPENDTHRIFT CLUB of Siena (Circle 7, "Squanderers") (*Inf.* 29.124–32): **Stricca**, most likely of the Salimbeni family, is accused of consuming his inheritance with reckless abandon; **Niccolò** de' Salimbeni, perhaps the brother of Stricca, is "credited" with introducing the clove (an expensive spice) into Sienese cuisine (according to Benvenuto, he introduced the extravagant practice of roasting game on a bed of cloves); **Caccia** d'Asciano, who was apparently forced to sell a vineyard and other holdings as a result of his profligate ways; and **Abbagliato** (a nickname, meaning "dazed," for Bartolommeo dei Folcacchieri), once fined for drinking in a tavern, who later played a leading role in Sienese and regional politics. In Benvenuto's entertaining account, this "club" was made up of rich young men (thought to number twelve in all) who pooled their funds to throw lavish banquets once or twice a month in a rented palace (they marked the end of a feast by tossing gold and silver utensils out the window).

GIANNI SCHICCHI AND MYRRHA (30) :: Like hogs released from their pen, two shades run wildly around the tenth pouch, sinking their teeth into other falsifiers. These are Gianni Schicchi and Myrrha, punished here (and tormenting others) for the sin of posing as another person for fraudulent reasons (*Inf.* 30.22–45). Gianni, who bites into the neck of Capocchio and drags the alchemist along the stone floor of the ditch, belonged to the Florentine Cavalcanti family. Renowned for his talent at mimicking others, Gianni once impersonated a dead man (Buoso Donati) in order to dictate a false will that named Buoso's nephew (Simone Donati) as principal heir; for himself, Gianni allotted a precious mule in addition to several hundred florins (Anonimo Fiorentino). Myrrha, consumed with desire for her father, King Cinyras of Cyprus, was so driven to despair that she wanted to hang herself. An old nurse, though horrified by the girl's incestuous longings, arranged for Myrrha to appear to be another young woman so that she could sleep with her father. The ruse worked until Cinyras one night brought in a lamp to view his lover; he immediately drew his sword to kill his daughter, but she escaped and, pregnant with her father's child, was eventually transformed into the tree that bears her name. The fruit of this father-daughter relationship was Adonis, who grew up to become the handsome lover of Venus (Ovid, *Metamorphoses* 10.298–532). Dante elsewhere equates the city of Florence with this "wicked and impious" Myrrha (*Epistola* 7.24).

MASTER ADAM, SINON THE GREEK, AND POTIPHAR'S WIFE (30) :: Adam and Sinon—counterfeiter and liar respectively—trade blows and then an escalating series of verbal barbs that illustrate the hostile attitude of shades toward one another in Lower Hell (*Inf.* 30.100–129). **Adam** was probably an Englishman who plied his illicit trade in late-thirteenth-century Italy, manufacturing florins (the prestigious medieval coin of Florence) containing only twenty-one carats of gold each instead of the standard twenty-four. Florins (*fiorini*), which entered circulation in 1252, were so named for having a lily (*fiore* means "flower") stamped on one side, while the other side bore an image of John the Baptist, patron saint of Florence (*Inf.* 30.74). Adam practiced his fraudulent craft in the service of the Guidi counts (the brothers Guido, Alessandro, and Aghinolfo), whose castle of Romena was located in the mountainous Casentino region (east of Florence). When Florentine authorities uncovered the counterfeiting racket in 1281, they promptly arrested Adam and burned him alive, as Sinon sarcastically recalls (*Inf.* 30.109–11). Adam now suffers in Hell from a severe case of dropsy, which causes his body (from the groin up) to resemble a lute, a musical instrument with a large, rounded base and a narrow fingerboard (*Inf.* 30.49–54). The disease also makes Adam experience unbearable thirst, though there is one thing he desires even more than water: to see among the falsifiers (and presumably take revenge on) those responsible for his damnation as a counterfeiter—that is, the three brothers, one of whom (he has heard) is already present in the tenth ditch (*Inf.* 30.76–90).

Sinon, a Greek participant in the Trojan War known to Dante from Virgil's *Aeneid* (2.57–198), earned his place in the pit of the falsifiers for telling a devastating lie: claiming to have escaped from his Greek comrades before they left Troy (he says they planned to sacrifice him in return for a safe voyage home), Sinon convinces the Trojans that the Greeks built a large wooden horse to placate the goddess (Athena), whose statue ULYSSES AND DIOMEDES (above) had stolen from Troy. The Trojans believe Sinon and think to protect Troy by bringing the horse inside the city walls; this enables the Greeks (hidden inside the horse) to accomplish by fraud what they had failed to bring about by force alone: the destruction of Troy.

Also seated close to Master Adam and reeking, like Sinon, from a feverish sweat, is "the lying woman who accused Joseph" (*Inf.* 30.97). This biblical liar, commonly known as **Potiphar's wife**, repeatedly attempted to seduce Joseph (son of Jacob and Rachel), whom Potiphar, chief captain of Pharaoh's army, had bought to serve in his house. One day when Joseph refused her sexual advances, she complained to the men of the house that he had attempted to sleep with her; Potiphar believed his wife (she offered as proof a piece of Joseph's clothing that she herself had taken when she tried to seduce him) and had Joseph thrown into prison (Genesis 39).

Allusions

MORE FRAUD: THEFT (24–25), FRAUDULENT COUN-
SEL (26–27), DIVISIVENESS (28), FALSIFICATION
(29–30) :: Included among Virgil's catalog of fraudulent offenses
in *Inferno* 11 are theft, falsifying, and "similar garbage" (59–60)—the
sins that are punished in the final four ditches of circle eight. With the
thieves appearing in the seventh pit and the falsifiers in the tenth, the
"similar garbage" must by default fill up ditches eight and nine. Divisive individuals—sowers of scandal and discord—are tormented in the
ninth ditch, and the shades punished in the eighth pit (hidden within
tongues of fire) are traditionally thought of as "evil counselors," based
on the damnation of Guido da Montefeltro (*Inf.* 27.116). A more accurate description, consistent with both the *contrapasso* of the tonguelike flames and the Ulysses episode in *Inferno* 26, in addition to Guido's
appearance in *Inferno* 27, might be the use of rhetoric—understood as
eloquence aimed at persuasion—by talented individuals for insidious
ends. Rhetoric, according to a classical tradition familiar to Dante, is
essential for civilized life when used wisely. However, eloquence *without*
wisdom, far worse even than wisdom without eloquence, is an evil that
can "corrupt cities and undermine the lives of men" (Cicero, *On Invention* 1.2.3).

Dante defines the concept of **contrapasso** in his presentation of
divisive shades: as they divided institutions, communities, and families in life, so these figures are physically (and repeatedly) sliced apart
for eternity in Hell (*Inf.* 28.139–42). The *contrapasso* for the thieves, on
the other hand, is arguably the most conceptually sophisticated of the
poem. Their dramatic transformations between human and reptilian
forms suggest that one's hold on one's identity is tenuous, that no possession, no matter how personal, is safe in the realm of theft. Slightly
less subtle is the *contrapasso* in the tenth and final pit of circle eight
for the falsifiers, whose corrupting influence on metals (alchemists),
money (counterfeiters), identity (imposters), and truth (liars) is reflected in their diseased bodies and minds.

INCARNATIONAL PARODY (25) :: The second transformation
of the thieves, in which a human and a six-footed serpent fuse into a

grotesque new form that is "neither two nor one" ("né due né uno"; *Inf.* 25.69), is likely intended as a parody of the Incarnation. This doctrine, established at the Council of Chalcedon in 451 after years of acrimonious debate among theologians, states that Christ is both human and divine, with each nature complete in its own right. Christ, who, along with the Virgin Mary, is never named in the *Inferno*, therefore comprises "two natures in one person." It is only natural for this theologically correct formulation to be parodied in Hell, perhaps by the hybrid creatures (Minotaur, Centaurs, Harpies) as well as by the conjoined thieves.

LUCAN AND OVID (25) :: Lucan and Ovid, together with Homer, Horace, and Virgil, make up the elite group of CLASSICAL POETS in Limbo (Circle 1) who welcome Dante as one of their own (*Inf.* 4.100–102). Here Dante interrupts his extraordinary description of a man and a reptile exchanging forms to boast that his verses surpass those of Lucan and Ovid, who wrote of merely unidirectional transformations (*Inf.* 25.94–102). Lucan, for example, tells how Sabellus, a soldier fighting in the Roman civil war, liquefies into a small pool of gore after being bitten by a snake in the Libyan desert, and how another unfortunate soldier, Nasidius, falls victim to a serpent's venom as his body swells into a featureless mass (*Pharsalia* 9.762–804). Ovid's Cadmus, brother of Europa and founder of Thebes, is transformed into a snake at the end of his life for slaying a serpent sacred to Mars (*Metamorphoses* 3.28–98, 4.571–603). Arethusa is a nymph transformed into a fountain (by Diana) to avoid the amorous advances of Alpheus, a river-god in human form who then reverts to his watery nature and thus succeeds in merging with Arethusa before the earth opens up and she plunges into the cavernous underworld (*Metamorphoses* 5.572–641).

ELIJAH'S CHARIOT (26) :: In the eighth pit of circle eight, Dante compares the flames that conceal the shades of the damned to the chariot that carried the prophet Elijah to the heavens (*Inf.* 26.34–42; 4 Kings 2:11–12). As "he who was avenged by bears" (*Inf.* 26.34)—that is, Elisha: two bears killed the boys who had mocked him (4 Kings 2:23–24)—could follow Elijah's ascent only by watching the fireball high in the sky, so Dante sees the flames but not the human forms they envelop.

ETEOCLES AND POLYNICES (26) :: Dante compares the twinned flame concealing the shades of Ulysses and Diomedes to the divided flame that rose from the funeral pyre containing the corpses of Eteocles and Polynices (*Inf.* 26.52–54). These twin brothers were sons of Jocasta and Oedipus, the king of Thebes, who prayed that Eteocles and Polynices would be forever enemies after they forced him to abdicate and leave the city. This prayer-curse came to fruition when, after the brothers had agreed to take turns ruling Thebes, Eteocles refused to give up power: Polynices enlisted the aid of King Adrastus of Argos, thus initiating the war of the SEVEN AGAINST THEBES (Circle 7, "Capaneus"; see also Circle 8, pouch 4, "Soothsayers"). After the brothers killed one another in combat, their bodies were placed together in a single pyre, but their mutual hatred was so intense, even after death, that the rising flame divided in two (Statius, *Thebaid* 12.429–35).

SICILIAN BULL (27) :: Dante compares the confusing sounds initially issuing from the flame concealing Guido da Montefeltro to the bellowing of the Sicilian bull (*Inf.* 27.7–15), a torture device built by the craftsman Perillus to gain the favor of Phalaris, a tyrant of Agrigentum in Sicily (ca. 570–554 BCE). The groans and screams of victims roasted within this hollow bronze statue (it was heated by fires placed underneath) would from the outside mimic the bellowing of cattle. Fittingly, the tyrant, "cherishing the invention and loathing the inventor," performed one just act in his life by making the bull's maker its first victim (Orosius, *History* 1.20.1–4).

ROMAGNA (27) :: Guido da Montefeltro's native land is the mountainous district that lies north of Urbino at the southern edge of the Romagna region. When Guido asks if current inhabitants of the area (roughly corresponding to the eastern portion of today's Emilia-Romagna region) are experiencing peace or war (*Inf.* 27.25–30), Dante's response is not reassuring. The absence of overt hostilities, Dante remarks, does not change the fact that war has always raged—and still does—in the hearts of the area's tyrants (*Inf.* 27.37–54): the "eagle of Polenta" (the powerful Polenta family) continues to rule over Ravenna and has expanded its wingspan southward along the coast to cover the

town of Cervia as well; the inland city of Forlì, which Guido successfully defended against French and Guelph troops (sent by Pope Martin
IV) in 1282, is now subdued by the "green paws" of the Ordelaffi family (whose coat of arms bore a green lion); the old and new mastiffs,
Malatesta and Malatestino da Verrucchio (father and step-brother of
Gianciotto and PAOLO [Circle 2, "Francesca and Paolo"]), still sink
their teeth into Rimini, as seen in their murder of Montagna de' Parci-
tati, head of the coastal city's Ghibelline party; and Maghinardo Pagani,
the "lion cub of the white lair" (his family insignia was a blue lion in
a white field), who fought as a Ghibelline in Romagna but a Guelph in
Tuscany, controls Faenza and Imola, towns on the Lamone and San-
terno rivers respectively. In 1300 the city of Cesena, located along the
Savio river between the plain and the mountain range, politically reflects its geographic position by hovering somewhere between liberty
and tyranny (as a relatively free commune ruled by Guido's cousin, Ga-
lasso da Montefeltro).

BATTLES IN SOUTHERN ITALY (28) :: So horrible is the
sight of the bloodied and mangled sowers of discord in the ninth pit
of circle eight that the combined carnage produced by battles fought in
Apulia—standing for the entire southern portion of continental Italy—
cannot match it (*Inf.* 28.7–21). The Romans (here called Trojans, after
their legendary ancestors) caused considerable bloodletting in their
wars against the Samnites (343–290 BCE) and the Tarentines (280–
275 BCE); fortune later turned against Rome when, as reported by Orosius (*History* 4.16.5) and Livy (*Roman History* 23.12.1–2), they suffered
such heavy losses at Cannae during the Second Punic War (218–201
BCE) that the victorious Hannibal sent to Carthage a large quantity of
gold rings taken from the hands of slain Roman knights and senators.
Greek and Muslim troops were the primary victims of battles fought
on behalf of the church by Robert Guiscard (ca. 1015–1085), a military
adventurer who brought southern Italy under Norman rule. Closer to
Dante's day, sovereignty over southern Italy was contested between the
troops of Charles of Anjou (supported by the church) and forces loyal
to MANFRED (Circle 6, "Guelphs and Ghibellines"), son of Emperor
Frederick II and ruler of the Kingdom of Sicily: the betrayal of Apulian

barons at Ceperano allowed Charles's army to pass unchallenged into the kingdom and to defeat Manfred at the battle of Benevento in 1266; two years later, at the battle of Tagliacozzo, Charles defeated Conradin (Manfred's nephew) by taking the counsel of his general, Érard ("Alardo") de Valéry, to unleash reserve forces (concealed behind a hill) just when the battle appeared to be lost.

FRA DOLCINO (28) :: Mohammed tells Dante to warn Fra Dolcino that, if he fails to stock up on food before winter arrives, it won't be long before he joins the sowers of discord in Hell (*Inf.* 28.55–60). Dolcino de' Tornielli of Novara (in Piedmont, west of Milan), son of a priest, became head of the Apostolic Brothers (a heretical sect) after Gerardo Segarelli of Parma, who founded the group in 1260, was burned alive by the Inquisition in 1300. Inspired by what they believed was the spiritual message of the original apostles (to live in poverty and preach the gospel), the sect was accused of heretical ideas and practices, such as the communal sharing of goods and women, and came to justify violent actions by demonizing its opponents. Dolcino and his followers established a stronghold in the Alps after POPE CLEMENT V (Circle 8, pouch 3) launched a crusade against them in 1305 and recruited fighters from Novara and other towns to root out the heretics. The Dolcinites, as they were called, held out for over a year until, forced by imminent starvation to make a last stand, they were nearly all killed or taken prisoner in 1307. Dolcino was captured together with his companion, Margaret of Trent, a woman known for her beauty and said to be Dolcino's mistress; after Fra Dolcino, his body horribly mutilated, had been paraded through the streets in a wagon, he and Margaret were burned at the stake.

THE PLAGUE AT AEGINA (29) :: Dante believes the falsifiers, whose shade-bodies are wracked by various infirmities and languish in piles along the floor of the tenth and final pit of circle eight, provide a spectacle even more wretched than plague-stricken Aegina (*Inf.* 29.58–66). Ovid recounts how Juno punished this island, named after a nymph whom Jupiter had loved, by unleashing a merciless pestilence (*Metamorphoses* 7.517–660). The malignant air, dense and sultry, infected the fields and waters and killed off the area's dogs, birds, livestock, and other animals. The plague then struck the human population (beginning with the farmers), causing dreadful suffering in its victims: "First of all the inner organs of the victim became burning hot: a flushed skin and panting breath were symptoms of internal fever. The tongue was rough and swollen, dry lips gaped open to catch breaths of the warm air, as men gaspingly tried to gulp in an atmosphere heavy with pollution" (7.554–57). Distraught by the decimation of his fellow citizens, Aeacus (the son of Aegina by Jupiter) pleaded with his divine father to restore the city's population by providing as many people as there were ants in a long column he saw winding its way along the trunk of a tall oak tree. After waking from a dream in which the ants grew and morphed into full grown humans, Aeacus heard voices in the palace and then saw that Jupiter had complied with his request. He named the new men Myrmidons after the Greek word (*myrmekes*) for ants (7.614–54).

ATHAMAS AND HECUBA (30) :: Dante compares the insane behavior of the impersonators Gianni Schicchi and Myrrha to stories of madness—one involving Thebans, the other Trojans—in classical literature (*Inf.* 30.1–27). Enraged at Jupiter's affair with Semele (Bacchus was their offspring), Juno, who had already caused Semele's death (she was incinerated after Juno, disguised as a trusted nurse, convinced her to have Jupiter appear in all his godly splendor), struck other members of Semele's Theban family: at the goddess's command, Tisiphone, one of the FURIES (Circle 5), poisoned the mind of King **Athamas**, Semele's brother-in-law, so that he believed his wife (Ino) and their two sons to be a lioness and cubs; after Athamas attacked them (killing one infant son, Learchus), Ino also lost her wits and, carrying the other child in her arms, leapt from a cliff into the roiling sea (Ovid, *Metamorphoses* 4.464–530). The example of Trojan madness is **Hecuba**, wife of King Priam, whose grief and fury so warped her mind that she began to bark like a dog when, following the destruction of Troy, she witnessed the death of her daughter Polyxena and came upon the corpse of POLYDORUS, her youngest son (Circle 7). Polyxena, who with her mother had been taken captive by the victorious Greeks, was slain as a sacrificial offering to the shade of Achilles, while Polydorus was killed by Polymnestor, king of Thrace, in whose care Priam had placed his son. Hecuba avenged her son's murder by gouging out Polymnestor's eyes. Pelted with rocks and weapons thrown by a crowd of Thracians, Hecuba responded with growls and bites; having lost her human voice, she could only express her grief by barking and howling (Ovid, *Metamorphoses* 13.399–575).

Significant Verses

gridando: "Togli, Dio, ch'a te le squadro!" (*Inf.* 25.3)
shouting: "Take these, God, I point them at you!"

Vedi che già non se' né due né uno (*Inf.* 25.69)
Look how already you're neither two nor one

fatti non foste a viver come bruti,
ma per seguir virtute e canoscenza (*Inf.* 26.119–20)
you weren't made to live like beasts,
but to follow virtue and knowledge

Io fui uom d'arme, e poi fui cordigliero (*Inf.* 27.67)
I was a man of arms, and then I was one who wore the cord

ed eran due in uno e uno in due (*Inf.* 28.125)
and they were two in one and one in two

Cosí s'osserva in me lo contrapasso (*Inf.* 28.142)
Thus you observe in me the contrapasso

Io vidi un, fatto a guisa di lëuto (*Inf.* 30.49)
I saw one who was shaped like a lute

Study Questions

1 :: How do the transformations of the thieves relate to the sin of theft?

2 :: Look closely at Dante's language in his claim to superiority over Lucan and Ovid based on his bidirectional transformation in

which man and reptile exchange forms (*Inf.* 25.94–102). What might this passage imply about Dante's participation in the realm of theft?

3 :: Why does Dante take Ulysses' story so personally (see *Inf.* 26.19–24)? What similarities and differences do you see between Dante and Ulysses?

4 :: What similarities and differences exist between Ulysses (*Inferno* 26) and Guido da Montefeltro (*Inferno* 27)? What is the sin for which they are both punished as tongues of fire in the eighth ditch of circle eight?

5 :: Some characters in Hell, such as FRANCESCA (Circle 2) and PIER DELLA VIGNA (Circle 7), tell stories directly related to their sin, while others—FARINATA (Circle 6), BRUNETTO (Circle 7)—discuss topics that seem to have little or no bearing on the sins for which they are condemned. Make the case for or against the view that Ulysses' tale of his final voyage indicates his sin.

6 :: Why do you think Dante selects Bertran de Born, the decapitated poet in the pit of the sowers of discord, to demonstrate and name the concept of *contrapasso*, the logical relationship between the sin and its punishment (*Inf.* 28.139–42)?

7 :: How do you understand the *contrapasso* for the falsifiers (*Inferno* 29–30)? That is, why does their punishment consist of diseased bodies and minds?

Circle 9: Treachery

INFERNO 31–34

TOWERING OVER the inner edge of circle eight are Giants, one of whom (Antaeus) lowers Dante and Virgil onto the frozen surface of Cocytus, the ninth circle of Hell. Embedded in separate regions of the ice are those who betrayed kin (Caina), homeland or political party (Antenora), guests (Ptolomea), and benefactors (Judecca). After kicking one of the political traitors hard in the face, Dante learns that this man (Bocca) betrayed the Florentine Guelphs at Montaperti. In the same region Dante finds Count Ugolino gnawing on the skull of Archbishop Ruggieri, whose cruelty caused Ugolino (with his sons and grandsons) to die of hunger. Fra Alberigo informs Dante that souls of those who betray their guests arrive in Hell even while their bodies continue to live on earth. In Judecca, at the very center of Hell, Dante sees Lucifer. Much larger than the Giants, he has three hideous faces and six huge, batlike wings that generate the winds needed to keep the lake frozen. Two mouths, one on each side, chew on Caesar's assassins, Brutus and Cassius, while the middle mouth engulfs Judas, the betrayer of Jesus. Virgil carries Dante down the shaggy body of Lucifer, making sure to flip over and climb once they have passed through the center of the earth. Dante then follows Virgil along a trail through the other half of the globe until he is able to see again the stars.

Encounters

GIANTS (31) :: The Giants physically connect circles eight and nine: standing on the floor of circle nine (or perhaps on a ledge above the bottom of Hell), the Giants tower over the inner edge of circle eight with the upper halves of their immense bodies. From a distance, in fact, Dante initially mistakes the Giants for actual towers (*Inf.* 31.19–45). Anticipating the even larger figure of Lucifer, Dante's Giants—drawn from both biblical and classical stories—are archetypal examples of defiant rebels. **Nimrod**, described in the Bible as a "stout hunter before the Lord" (Genesis 10:9), was viewed as a Giant in the Middle Ages. According to the biblical account, people in the region ruled by Nimrod (Babylon and other cities in the land of Sennaar) planned to build a tower that would reach to Heaven; God showed his displeasure by scattering the people and destroying the unity of their language so they could no longer understand one another's speech (Genesis 11:1–9).

Dante, following tradition, places the blame for this linguistic confusion on Nimrod, whose own language is now as incomprehensible to others as their languages are to him (*Inf.* 31.67–69, 76–81). In his physical description of Nimrod, Dante reinforces the association of the Giants with the ruinous consequences of pride: first, by comparing the size of Nimrod's face to the pine cone at Saint Peter's in Rome (*Inf.* 31.58–59), Dante perhaps means to draw an unflattering parallel with the current pope, BONIFACE VIII (Circle 8, pouch 3); and second, the word Dante uses (*perizoma*) to convey how the inner bank of circle eight covers the lower half of the Giants' bodies like an "apron" (*Inf.* 31.61–62) is an unusual term (of Greek origin) likely familiar to Dante's readers from a biblical verse describing the shame of Adam and Eve following their disobedience in the Garden of Eden: "And the eyes of them both were opened: and when they perceived themselves to be naked, they sewed together fig leaves, and made themselves aprons [*perizomata*]" (Genesis 3:7).

In their passage from circle eight to circle nine, Dante and Virgil view two other Giants, both from the classical tradition. **Ephialtes** was one of the Giants who fought against Jove and the other Olympian gods (*Inf.* 31.91–96). Ephialtes and his twin brother Otus (they were sons of Neptune and Iphimedia, wife of the Giant Aloeus) attempted to scale Mount Olympus and dethrone the gods by stacking Mount Pelion on top of Mount Ossa in Macedonia (*Aeneid* 6.582–84); they were killed, according to Servius's well-known medieval commentary on Virgil's *Aeneid*, with arrows shot by Apollo and Diana. Note Ephialtes' strong reaction to Virgil's statement that another Giant, Briareus, has an even more ferocious appearance (*Inf.* 31.106–11). Like the other Giants who challenged the gods, Ephialtes is immobilized by chains in Dante's Hell. **Antaeus**, who can speak, is probably unfettered because he was born after his brothers waged war against the gods. He is therefore able to lift Dante and Virgil and deposit them on the floor of the ninth and final circle of Hell (*Inf.* 31.130–45). To secure this assistance, Virgil entices Antaeus with the prospect of continued fame (upon Dante's return to the world) based on the Giant's formidable reputation. Here Dante's source is Lucan, who recounts how Antaeus, a fearsome child of Earth whose strength was replenished from contact with his mother, feasted on lions and slaughtered farmers and travelers around his cavernous dwelling in North Africa until he met his match in Hercules. The hero and the Giant engaged in a wrestling contest, which Hercules finally won by lifting Antaeus off the ground and squeezing him to death (*Pharsalia* 4.593–653). The Giant's fatal encounter with Hercules is recalled not by Virgil in his plea for Antaeus's help (*Inf.* 31.115–29) but by the narrator (*Inf.* 31.132). Virgil, however, is sure to reiterate Lucan's suggestion that the Giants might in fact have defeated the gods had Antaeus been present at the battle of PHLEGRA (Circle 7, "Capaneus") (*Inf.* 31.119–21).

ALBERTI BROTHERS AND OTHER TRAITORS AGAINST KIN (3 2) :: As he walks along the frozen surface of the ninth circle, Dante's attention is drawn to two figures at his feet who are locked chest to chest in the ice. When they raise their heads toward Dante, tears first roll down their faces and then freeze in their eye sockets, causing the two shades to butt one another like rams (*Inf.* 32.40–51). Dante learns from another frozen traitor that the angry pair are brothers: following the death of their father, Count Alberto of Mangona (who owned castles near Florence in the Bisenzio river valley), the Ghibelline **Napoleone** and the Guelph **Alessandro** killed one another (sometime between 1282 and 1286) because of a dispute over their inheritance. Dante is told that no one is more fitting than these two for punishment in Caina (where traitors against kin are tormented): not **Mordred**, who betrayed his uncle, King Arthur, by staging a coup d'état and whose body was pierced (so that sunlight shone through it) by Arthur's lance (*Inf.* 32.61–62); not Vanni dei Cancellieri, nicknamed **Focaccia**, a white Guelph from Pistoia who killed his father's cousin (a Pistoian black Guelph), thus giving rise to a cycle of factional violence that eventually made its way to FLORENCE (Circle 3, "Florentine Politics") (*Inf.* 32.63); and not **Sassol Mascheroni**, of the Florentine Toschi family, who, apprehended after murdering a cousin to take his inheritance, was rolled through the streets of Florence in a barrel full of nails and then beheaded (*Inf.* 32.63–66).

The speaker, who has lost both his ears to the cold, is Alberto (or Umberto) **Camiscion** (*Inf.* 32.68), a member of the Pazzi family of Valdarno, who was reported to have murdered his kinsman. One early commentator (Anonimo Fiorentino) says Camiscion rode up to his cousin Ubertino on horseback and stabbed him repeatedly in order to take possession of castles the two held in common. Camiscion now awaits the arrival of another kinsman, **Carlino** (*Inf.* 32.69), who is still alive in 1300 but will earn his place in the sector of circle nine reserved for traitors against party or homeland when (in 1302) he betrays exiled white Guelphs by accepting a bribe to surrender the castle of Piantravigne (where the exiles take refuge) to the Florentine black Guelphs.

BOCCA DEGLI ABATI AND OTHER POLITICAL TRAITORS (3 2) :: Dante certainly feels no remorse for kicking a shade hard in the face once he learns the identity of the political traitor (*Inf.* 32.73–78). The offended shade immediately piques Dante's interest by alluding to Montaperti (near Siena), site of the legendary battle in 1260 in which Florentine Guelphs were routed by Ghibelline forces that included, among exiles from Florence, FARINATA DEGLI UBERTI (Circle 6). The shade's identity remains concealed, even as Dante tries to elicit it by tearing out chunks of his hair, until another traitor in the ice calls out the wretch's name: Bocca promptly lives up to his name (*bocca* means "mouth") by identifying the informer along with four other traitors to political party or homeland (*Inf.* 32.112–23). **Bocca degli Abati** belonged to a Ghibelline family that remained in Florence after other Ghibellines were banished in 1258 for their role in a foiled plot. Pretending to fight on the side of the Guelphs (as part of the cavalry), Bocca betrayed his Guelph countrymen at a decisive moment in the battle: when German mercenary troops attacked in support of the Tuscan Ghibellines, he cut off the hand of the Guelph standard-bearer. Demoralized by Bocca's treachery and the loss of their flag, the Guelphs panicked and were roundly defeated.

Bocca avenges the disclosure of his identity by telling Dante not to stay silent about the one whose "tongue was so quick" (*Inf.* 32.113–17): **Buoso da Duera**, a Ghibelline leader from the northern Italian city of Cremona, disobeyed the orders of MANFRED (Circle 6, "Guelphs and Ghibellines") and betrayed his party when, bribed by "French money" (*Inf.* 32.115), he failed to engage the French troops of Charles of Anjou in 1265 as they marched south through Lombardy (and then took Parma) on their way to claim the Kingdom of Naples. Villani reports that the people of Cremona, enraged by Buoso's perfidy, wiped out the traitor's family lineage (*Chronicle* 8.4). Bocca then names four additional political traitors in the ice (*Inf.* 32.118–23). **Tesauro de' Beccheria**, abbot of Vallombrosa and papal legate to Alexander IV in Florence, was accused by the Florentine Guelphs of conspiring with the exiled Ghibellines in 1258; he confessed under torture and was promptly beheaded, for which the outraged pope excommunicated the entire city. **Gianni de' Soldanieri**, descendant of a noble Florentine Ghibelline family, switched to the Guelph side after the defeat of Manfred at Benevento in 1266 and helped lead a popular uprising against the Florentine Ghibelline rulers; Gianni was placed at the head of a provisional government, but the pope, suspicious of his motives for swapping allegiances, disapproved of the appointment, and Gianni was likely forced to flee Florence himself. **Ganelon**'s treason was legendary in the Middle Ages (among Dante's sources is the Old French *Song of Roland*). Sent by Charlemagne to demand of Marsilio, the Saracen king, that he either receive baptism or pay a tribute, Ganelon was instead induced to betray the Christian forces. In 778 he convinced Charlemagne to cross the Pyrenees into France and leave Roland (Charlemagne's nephew and Ganelon's stepson) with the rear guard of the army in Spain; ambushed by the Saracens at Roncevalles, Roland desperately sounded his horn, but Ganelon persuaded Charlemagne not to return to help (he said Roland often blew the horn while hunting) and thus completed his treachery as the entire rear guard was slain. Charlemagne later tried Ganelon, who was found guilty and pulled apart by four horses. **Tebaldello**, a Ghibelline from the Zambrasi family of Faenza, avenged a private grudge (a quarrel over two pigs, according to Benvenuto) by betraying the Ghibelline Lambertazzi family, who had taken refuge in Faenza after their expulsion from Bologna; early in the morning of November 13, 1280, Tebaldello "opened Faenza while it slept" (*Inf.* 32.123), thus allowing Bolognese Guelph enemies of the Lambertazzi to enter the city and slaughter them.

COUNT UGOLINO AND ARCHBISHOP RUGGIERI (32–33) :: There is perhaps no more grisly scene in all the *Inferno* than Dante's depiction of Ugolino eating the back of Ruggieri's head like a dog using its strong teeth to gnaw a bone (*Inf.* 32.124–32, 33.76–78). Dante emphasizes the hostility underlying Ugolino's cannibalism by recalling a similarly brutal scene from the classical tradition (*Inf.* 32.130–32): Tydeus, one of the SEVEN AGAINST THEBES (Circle 7, "Capaneus"; see also Circle 8, pouch 4, "Soothsayers," and pouch 8, "Eteocles and Polynices"), having been mortally wounded by Menalippus (and having returned the favor), calls for his enemy's head so that he can exact added revenge before succumbing to death (Statius, *Thebaid* 8.716–66). Ugolino's story, the longest single speech by one of the damned, is Dante's final dramatic representation in the *Inferno* of humankind's capacity for evil and cruelty. Aimed at explaining the scene of cannibalism in Hell, Ugolino's words are all the more powerful because he makes no attempt to exonerate himself of the crime (political treachery) for which he is condemned to eternal damnation. He instead wishes to defame his enemy and elicit compassion from his audience by recounting the brutal manner in which he and his innocent children were killed.

Count Ugolino della Gherardesca earned his place in Antenora, the realm of political traitors, for a series of betrayals against Pisa and the city's political leadership. Dante mentions only the reputed act of treason that eventually led to Ugolino's downfall: in an effort to appease hostile and powerful Guelph forces in Tuscany, Ugolino ceded Pisan castles to Florence and Lucca in 1285 (*Inf.* 33.85–86). However, early commentators and chroniclers describe other, even more damning examples of betrayals and shifting allegiances in the long political life of Count Ugolino. Born into a prominent Ghibelline family in Pisa, Ugolino switched to the Guelph side following their ascendancy in Tuscan politics and tried to install a Guelph government in Pisa in 1274–75. Unsuccessful in this attempt, he was imprisoned and later exiled. In 1284, several years after his return, Ugolino led Pisan forces in a naval battle against rival Genoa; despite his defeat, Ugolino was appointed *podestà* (political head) of Pisa, and his Guelph grandson, Nino Visconti, soon joined him in power as "captain of the people." It was in this period that Ugolino, out of political expediency, ceded the Pisan castles to Lucca and Florence, a decision that caused a rift between him and his grandson and between their Guelph followers.

Taking advantage of resurgent Ghibelline fortunes in Tuscany, Ugolino connived with the Pisan Ghibellines, led by **Archbishop Ruggieri degli Ubaldini**, nephew of the heretical CARDINAL OTTAVIANO DEGLI UBALDINI (Circle 6); Ugolino agreed to Ghibelline demands that Nino be driven from the city, an order that was carried out (with Ugolino purposefully absent from the city) in 1288. The traitor, however, was then himself betrayed: upon Ugolino's return to Pisa, Ruggieri incited the public against him (by cleverly exploiting Ugolino's previous "betrayal of the castles") and had the count arrested and imprisoned along with two sons (Gaddo and Uguiccione) and two grandsons (Anselmuccio and Nino). They were held in the tower for eight months until, with a change in the Ghibelline leadership of Pisa, it was decided to nail shut the door to the tower and to throw the key into the Arno. The prisoners starved to death, as Dante's Ugolino recalls, in a matter of days (*Inf.* 33.67–75).

FRA ALBERIGO AND BRANCA DORIA (33) :: Dante cleverly tricks a shade into revealing his identity by making a devious deal (*Inf.* 33.109–17): if he doesn't relieve the traitor's suffering (by removing ice—frozen tears—from the traitor's face) in exchange for this information, Dante says he should be sent to the very bottom of Hell! Dante thus learns that the soul of Fra Alberigo is in Hell even as his body, in 1300, the year of the journey, still lives on earth (he is thought to have died in 1307). **Fra Alberigo**, of the ruling Guelph family of Faenza (near Ravenna), was a JOVIAL FRIAR (Circle 8, pouch 6), a member of a military-religious order established with the goal of making peace (within families and cities) but soon better known for decadence and corruption. A close relative, Manfred, plotted against Alberigo for political power, and one day, when tensions escalated, slapped him hard (Benvenuto); Fra Alberigo's cruel response well earned him a place among the traitors in Hell. Pretending that the altercation was forgotten, Alberigo invited Manfred and his son to a sumptuous banquet; when, at the end of the meal, the host gave the signal ("Bring the fruit!"), armed servants emerged from behind a curtain and slaughtered the guests, much to the delight of Alberigo.

Drawing Dante's attention to a shade next to him in the ice, Alberigo explains that the souls of those who betray their guests descend immediately to Ptolomea as their bodies are possessed by demons (*Inf.* 33.124–33). Thus Dante learns that the soul of **Branca Doria**, whose body on earth still "eats and drinks and sleeps and wears clothes," has already inhabited this sector of the ninth circle for many years (*Inf.*

33.134–47). Branca's soul arrived here even before the soul of his father-in-law, MICHELE ZANCHE (Circle 8, pouch 5, "Ciampolo and Other Barrators"), arrived in the boiling pitch of circle eight, where corrupt bureaucrats and politicians are punished. In 1275 (or, some believe, 1290) Branca invited Michele, who was a judge and governor in Sardinia, to a banquet where, accompanied by a nephew or cousin, he murdered him. Not only was Branca Doria (born ca. 1233 into a prominent Ghibelline family of Genoa) living at the time of this journey to the afterlife, but documents suggest he lived into his nineties and was still alive in 1325, four years after Dante's death.

LUCIFER (WITH BRUTUS, JUDAS, AND CASSIUS) (34) :: Lucifer, Satan, Dis, Beelzebub—Dante throws every name in the book at the Devil, who was once the most beautiful angel (Lucifer means "light-bearer") and then, following his rebellion against God, became the source of evil and sorrow in the world, beginning with his corruption of Eve and Adam in the Garden of Eden (Genesis 3). Dante's Lucifer is a parodic composite of his wickedness and the divine powers that punish him in Hell. As ugly as he once was beautiful, Lucifer is the wretched emperor of Hell, whose tremendous size (he dwarfs even the Giants) stands in contrast with his limited autonomy: his flapping wings generate the wind that keeps the lake frozen, while his three mouths chew on the shade-bodies of three archtraitors, the gore mixing with tears gushing from Lucifer's three sets of eyes (*Inf.* 34.53–57). Lucifer's three faces, each a different color (black, red, whitish yellow), parody the doctrine of the Trinity: three complete persons (Father, Son, Holy Spirit) in one divine nature—the Divine Power, Highest Wisdom, and Primal Love that created the GATE OF HELL (Periphery of Hell) and, by extension, the entire realm of eternal damnation. With the top half of his body towering over the ice, Lucifer resembles the Giants and other half-visible figures; after Dante and Virgil have passed through the center of the earth, their perspective changes and Lucifer appears upside-down, with his legs sticking up in the air. This final image of Lucifer thus resembles the sight of the simonists, in particular POPE NICHOLAS III (Circle 8, pouch 3).

Eternally eaten by Lucifer's three mouths are (from left to right facing Lucifer) Brutus, Judas, and Cassius (*Inf.* 34.61–67). **Brutus** and

Cassius, stuffed feetfirst into the jaws of Lucifer's black and whitish yellow faces respectively, are punished in this lowest region for their assassination of JULIUS CAESAR (44 BCE) (Circle 1, "Virtuous Pre- and Non-Christians"), the founder of the Roman Empire that Dante viewed as an essential part of God's plan for human happiness. Both Brutus and Cassius fought on the side of Pompey in the civil war. Following Pompey's defeat at Pharsalia (48 BCE), Caesar pardoned them and invested both men with high civic offices. Cassius, however, continued to harbor resentment against Caesar's dictatorship and enlisted the aid of Brutus in a conspiracy to kill Caesar and reestablish the republic. They succeeded in assassinating Caesar but their political-military ambitions were thwarted by Octavian (later Augustus) and Antony at Philippi (42 BCE): Cassius, defeated by Antony and thinking (wrongly) that Brutus had been defeated by Octavian, had himself killed by a servant; Brutus in turn lost a subsequent battle and took his life as well. For Dante, Brutus and Cassius's betrayal of Julius Caesar, their benefactor and the world's supreme secular ruler, complements Judas Iscariot's betrayal of Jesus, the Christian man-god, in the Gospels. **Judas**, one of the twelve apostles, struck a deal to betray Jesus for thirty pieces of silver and fulfilled his treacherous role (foreseen by Jesus at the Last Supper) when he identified Jesus to the authorities with a kiss; regretting this betrayal, which would lead to Jesus's death, Judas returned the silver and hanged himself (Matthew 26:14–16, 26:21–25, 26:47–49, 27:3–5). Suffering even more than Brutus and Cassius, Dante's Judas is placed headfirst inside Lucifer's central mouth, with his back skinned by the devil's claws (*Inf.* 34.58–63).

Allusions

TREACHERY: CAINA (32), ANTENORA (32–33), PTOLO-MEA (33), JUDECCA (34) :: Dante divides circle nine, the circle of treachery—defined as fraudulent acts between individuals who share special bonds of love and trust (*Inf.* 11.61–66)—into four regions. **Caina** is named after the biblical Cain (first child of Adam and Eve), who slew his brother Abel out of envy after God showed appreciation for Abel's sacrificial offering but not for Cain's (Genesis 4:1–17); condemned to a vagabond existence, Cain later built a city (named after his son, Enoch) that for certain Christian theologians, notably Augustine (*City of God* 15), represented the evils of the earthly city. In the circle of the lustful, FRANCESCA (Circle 2) identified her husband, Gianciotto, who murdered her and Paolo (Gianciotto's brother), as a future inhabitant of Caina (*Inf.* 5.107).

The second region is named for the Trojan prince **Antenora**. While the classical sources, such as Homer's *Iliad*, present Antenora in a positive (or at least neutral) light as favoring the return of Helen to the Greeks for the good of Troy, medieval histories, commentaries, and romances view him as a "treacherous Judas" who plotted with the Greeks to destroy the city. Dante places in this region those who betrayed their political party or their homeland.

In the third zone of circle nine suffer those who betrayed friends or guests. **Ptolomea** is named after one or both of the following: Ptolemy, the captain of Jericho, who honored his father-in-law, the high priest Simon Maccabee (and two of Simon's sons) with a great feast and then murdered them (1 Maccabees 16:11–17), or Ptolemy XII, brother of Cleopatra, who arranged for the Roman general Pompey—seeking refuge following his defeat at the battle of Pharsalia (48 BCE)—to be murdered as soon as he stepped ashore. Dante displays his abhorrence of such crimes by devising a special rule for those who betray their guests: their souls descend immediately to Hell and their living bodies are possessed by demons when they commit these acts (*Inf.* 33.124–33).

Judecca, named after the apostle who betrayed Jesus (Judas Iscariot), is the innermost zone of the ninth and final circle of Hell. The term also hints at a manifestation of Christian prejudice (which Dante shares) against Judaism and Jews in the Middle Ages: it alludes to names—*Iudeca, Judaica*—for the area within certain cities (such as Venice) where Jews were forced to live, apart from the Christian population. Together with Judas in this region of Hell are others who, by betraying their masters or benefactors, committed crimes with great historical and societal consequences. Completely covered by the ice like "straw in glass," the shades are locked in various postures with no mobility or sound whatsoever (*Inf.* 34.10–15).

OTHER GIANTS (31) :: Although Dante and Virgil do not visit them, three other towering Giants are named in *Inferno* 31. **Briareus**, whom Virgil describes as equal in size to (but even more terrifying than) Ephialtes (*Inf.* 31.103–5), appears in Virgil's epic as a monster said to have one hundred arms and hands, with fire burning in his fifty mouths and chests; he was thus able to wield fifty shields and swords to defend himself against Jove's thunderbolts (*Aeneid* 6.287, 10.565–68). Statius merely describes Briareus as immense (*Thebaid* 2.596). Repeating Lucan's coupling of Tityus and Typhon as Giants inferior to Antaeus (*Pharsalia* 4.595–96), Virgil appeals to Antaeus's pride by "threatening" to go to them if Antaeus will not provide a lift down to circle nine (*Inf.* 31.124–26). **Tityus** is well represented in classical literature as a Giant whose attempted rape of Latona (mother of Apollo and Diana) earns him a gruesome fate in the underworld: a vulture continuously feeds on his immortal liver (Virgil, *Aeneid* 6.595–600; Ovid, *Metamorphoses* 4.457–58). **Typhon** was struck down by Jove's lightning and, depending on the version, buried under Sicily's volcanic Mount Etna (out of which he spews earth and fire; *Metamorphoses* 5.318–58) or under the island of Ischia in the Bay of Naples (*Aeneid* 9.715–16).

COCYTUS (32–34) :: Dante calls circle nine, a frozen lake, Cocytus (from Greek, meaning "to lament"). One of the rivers in the classical underworld, Cocytus is described by Virgil as a dark, deep pool of water that encircles a forest and into which pours sand spewed from a torrid whirlpool (*Aeneid* 6.131–32, 6.296–97, 6.323). In the Vulgate (the Latin Bible) Job explains that the wicked, though they often prosper in the world, at their death shall be received into the valley (or torrent) of Cocytus (Job 21:33).

Significant Verses

sappi che non son torri, ma giganti (*Inf.* 31.31)
know that they are not towers but giants

forte percossi 'l piè nel viso ad una (*Inf.* 32.78)
I struck my foot hard in the face of one of them

sí che l'un capo a l'altro era cappello (*Inf.* 32.126)
so that one head to the other was a hat

Poscia, piú che 'l dolor, poté 'l digiuno (*Inf.* 33.75)
then, stronger than grief was my hunger

al fondo de la ghiaccia ir mi convegna (*Inf.* 33.117)
may I go to the bottom of the ice

Lo 'mperador del doloroso regno (*Inf.* 34.28)
The emperor of the sorrowful kingdom

E quindi uscimmo a riveder le stelle (*Inf.* 34.139)
We then emerged to see again the stars

Study Questions

1 :: Why is the frozen lake in the lowest circle of Hell (Cocytus) a suitable place for the punishment of traitors? Describe the general *contrapasso* for treachery.

2 :: The Giants and Lucifer are proud figures who appear divided, with only the top halves of their bodies visible to Dante and Virgil. Similarly, half the bodies of Cassius, Judas, and Brutus are punished within Lucifer's massive jaws. Count Ugolino, on the other hand, is doubled with his mortal enemy, Archbishop Ruggieri. Think of other divided or doubled figures in the *Inferno* and how they might be part of Dante's web of pride, one of only two capital sins not assigned a circle in Hell.

3 :: Envy is the other capital sin not assigned its own circle in Dante's Hell. Are there particular characters, in the ninth circle or elsewhere in Hell, who are guilty of envy?

4 :: What might it mean for Dante to deny pride and envy their own circles in Hell?

5 :: Find examples in these cantos of Dante's participation in the sin of treachery.

6 :: Why do you think Dante singles out those who betray guests for the special "privilege" of going straight to Hell (Ptolomea) at the

moment of their sin—that is, while their bodies (possessed by devils) continue to inhabit the world (*Inf.* 33.124–33)?

7 :: Lucifer, with his three faces, is a perverse image of the Holy Trinity, the Christian doctrine of three complete persons (Father, Son, Holy Spirit) in a single divine nature. What other characters in Hell or aspects of the poem might serve as Trinitarian parodies? Why is it appropriate for Dante to present negative images of Christian doctrine, such as the Trinity and Incarnation, in Hell?

Changing Values?

AS A RELATIVELY PRIVILEGED European man of the late Middle Ages, Dante certainly shares, despite his intellect and imagination, views we might rightly consider unenlightened. These could include religious and ethnic intolerance as well as a reductive attitude toward gender and sexuality. In some cases—for instance, his economic positions and his advocacy of the empire (and opposition to more democratic, republican ideas)—he could be considered reactionary even for his own time and place.

While we might like to think of ourselves as intelligent, forward-looking individuals, what might our descendants say about us a century or two from now? What specific issues or attitudes do you think will change so much in the future that our current views may come to be seen as "medieval"?

ACKNOWLEDGMENTS

Complementing this book is a multimedia *Danteworlds* Web site. Provost Sheldon Ekland-Olson has led the way in promoting innovative scholarship and instructional technology at the University of Texas at Austin, and I am grateful to the College of Liberal Arts for providing grants that allowed me to transform the idea of *Danteworlds* into (virtual) reality. For the design, implementation, and maintenance of the Web site, I am indebted to the superb staff of Liberal Arts Instructional Technology Services, directed by Joe TenBarge: collaborating with Suloni Robertson (artist and graphic designer) and Gary Dickerson (site designer and programmer), I have experienced the pleasure and satisfaction of true teamwork. I thank Suloni for providing the map of Italy and the illustration of Dante's Hell.

I greatly appreciate the unfailing support of Daniela Bini, Douglas Biow, Antonella Olson, Cinzia Russi, and my other colleagues in the Department of French and Italian. I drew inspiration for the *Danteworlds* project from friends and fellow *dantisti* at biannual meetings of the council and editorial board of the Dante Society of America. For their collegiality and encouragement, I thank Giuseppe Mazzotta, Teodolinda Barolini, Nancy Vickers, Steven Botterill, Todd Boli, John Ahern, Brenda Schildgen, Christian Moevs, Susan Noakes, Rachel Jacoff, Regina Psaki, Peter Hawkins, Simon Gilson, Jan Ziolkowski, Richard Lansing, Olivia Holmes, and Dana Stewart.

Danteworlds also benefited from the support of the following scholars and teachers at the University of Texas at Austin and at other schools (universities, colleges, and high schools) who used the Web site in their classes or shared wisdom gained from their own research and teaching: Thomas Mussio, Jeffrey Schnapp, Peter Bondanella, Julia Bondanella, Carole Hamilton, Christopher Kleinhenz, Robert Hollander, Deborah Parker, Kevin Brownlee, Cosetta Gaudenzi, Elizabeth Cullingford, Elizabeth Richmond-Garza, Marjorie Woods, Coco Kishi, and Olin Bjork. I am extremely grateful to Alan Thomas at the University of Chicago Press and to the four scholars who read the book in manuscript form and provided specific suggestions for improving it. Joel Score was an ideal manuscript editor; he not only polished and enlivened my prose but also asked probing questions that helped me to clarify meaning without sacrificing accuracy. Responsibility for errors and infelicities of any kind lies with me alone.

Most of all I thank Helene Meyers, with whom I have shared laughter and tears during the past twenty years, for reminding me at crucial moments that *Danteworlds* was worth doing after all. Both the Web site and this book exist because of her.

References to Dante's works are taken from the following editions. Translations of the *Divine Comedy* are my own.

Convivio. Edited by Cesare Vasoli and Domenico De Robertis. In Dante Alighieri, *Opere minori*, vol. 2, bks. 1–2. Milan: Ricciardi, 1995.

Dante, *Monarchia.* Translated and edited by Prue Shaw. Cambridge: Cambridge University Press, 1995.

Dante, *De vulgari eloquentia.* Edited and translated by Steven Botterill. Cambridge: Cambridge University Press, 1996.

Dante's Il Convivio (The Banquet). Translated by Richard H. Lansing. New York: Garland, 1990.

La Divina Commedia. Edited by Giorgio Petrocchi. Turin: Einaudi, 1975.

Epistole. Edited by Arsenio Frugoni and Giorgio Brugnoli. In Dante Alighieri, *Opere minori*, vol. 3, bk. 2. Milan: Ricciardi, 1996.

"The Letter to Can Grande." In *Literary Criticism of Dante Alighieri*, translated and edited by Robert S. Haller, 95–111. Lincoln: University of Nebraska Press, 1973.

Vita nuova. Edited and translated by Dino S. Cervigni and Edward Vasta. Notre Dame, Ind.: University of Notre Dame Press, 1995.

References to the following early commentators of the *Divine Comedy* are taken from the database of the Dartmouth Dante Project (http://dante.dartmouth.edu): Jacopo della Lana (1324–28), L'Ottimo (1333), Anonimo Selmiano (1337?), Pietro Alighieri (1340–64?), Giovanni Boccaccio (1373–75), Benvenuto da Imola (1375–80), Francesco da Buti (1385–95), Anonimo Fiorentino (1400?), and Johannis de Serravale (1416–17). Translations are my own.

Biblical references are from *Biblia Sacra iuxta Vulgatam Clementinam*, 6th ed., edited by Alberto Colunga and Lorenzo Turrado (Madrid: Biblioteca de Autores Cristianos, 1982). Translations are from *The Holy Bible* (New York: Douay Bible House, 1941).

Other cited works are listed in the bibliography under "Classical and Medieval Sources."

BIBLIOGRAPHY

REFERENCE WORKS

Bosco, Umberto, ed. *Enciclopedia dantesca*. 6 vols. Rome: Istituto dell'Enciclopedia Italiana, 1970–78.

Brieger, Peter, Millard Meiss, and Charles S. Singleton, eds. *Illuminated Manuscripts of the "Divine Comedy."* Princeton: Princeton University Press, 1969.

Delmay, Bernard. *I personaggi della "Divina commedia": Classificazione e regesto*. Florence: Olschki, 1986.

Kleinhenz, Christopher, ed. *Medieval Italy: An Encyclopedia*. 2 vols. New York: Routledge, 2004.

Lansing, Richard, ed. *The Dante Enclyclopedia*. New York: Garland, 2000.

Merlante, Riccardo. *Il dizionario della "Commedia."* Bologna: Zanichelli, 1999.

Toynbee, Paget. *A Dictionary of Proper Names and Notable Matters in the Works of Dante*. Revised by Charles S. Singleton. Oxford: Clarendon Press, 1968.

BIOGRAPHIES AND GUIDES

Barbi, Michele. *Dante: Vita, opere, fortuna*. Florence: Sansoni, 1933. (Translated by Paul G. Ruggiers [Berkeley: University of California Press, 1954].)

Bemrose, Stephen. *A New Life of Dante*. Exeter, England: University of Exeter Press, 2000.

Bernardo, Aldo S., and Anthony L. Pellegrini. *Companion to Dante's "Divine Comedy."* Binghamton, N.Y.: Global Academic Publishing, 2006.

Boccaccio, Giovanni. *Vita di Dante*. Edited by Bruno Cagli. Rome: Avanzini e Torraca, 1965.

Gallagher, Joseph. *A Modern Reader's Guide to Dante's "The Divine Comedy."* Liguori, Mo.: Liguori, 1999.

Hawkins, Peter S. *Dante: A Brief History*. Oxford: Blackwell, 2006.

Hollander, Robert. *Dante: A Life in Works*. New Haven: Yale University Press, 2001.

Holmes, George. *Dante*. Oxford: Oxford University Press, 1980.

Kirkpatrick, Robin. *Dante: The "Divine Comedy": A Student Guide*. 2d ed. Cambridge: Cambridge University Press, 2004.

Lewis, R. W. B. *Dante*. New York: Viking Penguin, 2001.

Padoan, Giorgio. *Introduzione a Dante*. Florence: Sansoni, 1975.

Petrocchi, Giorgio. *Vita di Dante*. Rome: Laterza, 1983.

Quinones, Ricardo J. *Dante Alighieri*. Boston: Twayne, 1979.

Rubin, Harriet. *Dante in Love*. New York: Simon & Schuster, 2004.

Slade, Carole, ed. *Approaches to Teaching Dante's "Divine Comedy."* New York: Modern Language Association of America, 1982.

DANTE WEB SITES

Danteworlds: http://danteworlds.laits.utexas.edu/
Dante Online (Società Dantesca Italiana): http://www.danteonline.it/
Princeton Dante Project: http://etcweb.princeton.edu/dante/
Digital Dante: http://dante.ilt.columbia.edu/new/
The World of Dante: http://www3.iath.virginia.edu/dante/
Dante Society of America: http://www.dantesociety.org/
Dartmouth Dante Project: http://dante.dartmouth.edu/
Renaissance Dante in Print (1472–1629): http://www.italnet.nd.edu/Dante/

CLASSICAL AND MEDIEVAL SOURCES

Aquinas, Thomas. *Commentary on Aristotle's "Politics"* [In libros Politicorum Aristotelis Expositio]. Edited by R. M. Spiazzi. Turin: Marietti, 1951.
———. *Commentary on the "Nichomachean Ethics."* Translated by C. I. Litzinger. 2 vols. Chicago: Regnery, 1964.
———. *Summa theologiae.* Blackfriars edition. Translated by Thomas Gilby et al. 61 vols. New York: McGraw Hill, 1964–81.
Aristotle. *The Nichomachean Ethics.* Translated by H. Rackham. Cambridge: Harvard University Press, 1939.
———. *Physics.* Translated by Philip H. Wicksteed and Francis M. Cornford. 2 vols. Cambridge: Harvard University Press, 1957–60.
———. *The Politics.* Translated by H. Rackham. Cambridge: Harvard University Press, 1959.
Augustine. *The City of God.* Translated by G. E. McCracken et al. 7 vols. Cambridge, Harvard University Press, 1957–72.
———. *Confessions.* Translated by William Watts. 2 vols. 1912. Reprint, Cambridge: Harvard University Press, 1979.
Boethius. *The Consolation of Philosophy.* Translated by S. J. Tester. Cambridge: Harvard University Press, 1973.
Boniface VIII (pope). *Unam sanctam.* Translated by Brian Tierney. In *Sources of Medieval History,* 320–22. Vol. 1 of *The Middle Ages,* edited by Brian Tierney. 3d ed. New York: Knopf, 1978.
Cicero, Marcus Tullius. *De amicitia* [On Friendship]. Translated by William Armistead Falconer. 1927. Reprint, Cambridge: Harvard University Press, 1959.
———. *De finibus bonorum et malorum* [On Moral Ends]. Translated by H. Rackham. 2d ed. Cambridge: Harvard University Press, 1951.

———. *De inventione* [On Invention]. Translated by H. M. Hubbell. 1949. Reprint, Cambridge: Harvard University Press, 1976.

———. *De officiis* [On Duty]. Translated by Walter Miller. 1913. Reprint, Cambridge: Harvard University Press, 1938.

Gardiner, Eileen, ed. *Visions of Heaven and Hell before Dante.* New York: Italica Press, 1989.

Livy. *Roman History.* Translated by B. O. Foster et al. 14 vols. Cambridge: Harvard University Press, 1949–61.

Lucan. *Pharsalia* [The Civil War]. Translated by J. D. Duff. Cambridge: Harvard University Press, 1951.

Orosius. *Seven Books of History against the Pagans.* Translated by Roy J. Deferrari. Washington, D. C.: Catholic University of America, 1964.

Ovid. *Ars amatoria* [The Art of Love]. Translated by J. H. Mozley. 1929. Reprint, Cambridge: Harvard University Press, 1962.

———. *Fasti.* Translated by James George Frazer. 2d ed. Revised by G. P. Goold. Cambridge: Harvard University Press, 1989.

———. *Heroides.* Translated by Grant Showerman. 2d ed. Revised by G. P. Goold. 1977. Reprint, Cambridge: Harvard University Press, 1996.

———. *Metamorphoses.* Edited by B. A. van Proosdij. Leiden: E. J. Brill, 1982. (Translated by Mary M. Innes [Harmondsworth, England: Penguin, 1955].)

Pseudo-Bernardus Silvestris. *Commentary on the First Six Books of Virgil's "Aeneid."* Translated by Earl G. Schreiber and Thomas E. Maresca. Lincoln: University of Nebraska Press, 1979.

Statius. *Thebaid.* Edited by D. E. Hill. Leiden: E. J. Brill, 1983. (Translated by Charles Stanley Ross [Baltimore: Johns Hopkins University Press, 2004].)

Villani, Giovanni. *Nuova cronica.* Edited by Giuseppe Porta. 3 vols. Parma: Fondazione Pietro Bembo, 1990–91. (*Villani's Chronicle,* translated by Rose E. Selfe [London: Archibald Constable & Co., 1906].)

Virgil. *Aeneid.* Edited by R. A. B. Mynors. Oxford: Oxford University Press, 1969. (Translated by Allen Mandelbaum [Berkeley: University of California Press, 1981].)

———. *Eclogues.* Edited by R. A. B. Mynors. Oxford: Oxford University Press, 1969. (Translated by Guy Lee [Harmondsworth, England: Penguin, 1980].)

———. *Georgics.* Edited by R. A. B. Mynors. Oxford: Oxford University Press, 1969. (Translated by C. Day Lewis [Garden City, N.Y.: Anchor Books, 1964].)

Wilhelm, James J., ed. *Lyrics of the Middle Ages: An Anthology.* New York: Garland, 1990.

William of Conches. *Glosae in Iuvenalem.* Edited by Bradford Wilson. Paris: J. Vrin, 1980.

MODERN CRITICISM AND COMMENTARY

Selected works, with an emphasis on the Inferno *and Dante's cultural background.*

Anderson, William. *Dante the Maker.* New York: Crossroad, 1980.

Auerbach, Erich. *Dante, Poet of the Secular World.* Translated by Ralph Manheim. Chicago: University of Chicago Press, 1961.

———. "Figura." Translated by Ralph Manheim. In *Scenes from the Drama of European Literature: Six Essays.* New York: Meridian Books, 1959. 11–76.

———. *Literary Language and Its Public in Late Latin Antiquity and in the Middle Ages.* Translated by Ralph Manheim. 1965. Reprint, with a forward by Jan M. Ziolkowski, Princeton: Princeton University Press, 1993.

Baranski, Zygmunt G. *Dante e i segni: Saggi per una storia intellettuale di Dante Alighieri.* Naples: Liguori, 2000.

Bárberi Squarotti, Giorgio. *In nome di Beatrice e altre voci.* Turin: Genesi, 1989.

———. *L'ombra di Argo: Studi sulla "Commedia."* 3d ed. Turin: Genesi, 1988.

Barolini, Teodolinda. *Dante's Poets: Textuality and Truth in the "Comedy."* Princeton: Princeton University Press, 1984.

———. *The Undivine "Comedy": Detheologizing Dante.* Princeton: Princeton University Press, 1992.

Bloch, R. Howard. *Medieval Misogyny and the Invention of Western Romantic Love.* Chicago: University of Chicago Press, 1991.

Bloom, Harold, ed. *Dante's "Inferno."* New York: Chelsea House, 1996.

Boswell, John. *Christianity, Social Tolerance, and Homosexuality: Gay People in Western Europe from the Beginning of the Christian Era to the Fourteenth Century.* Chicago: University of Chicago Press, 1980.

Boyde, Patrick. *Dante Philomythes and Philosopher: Man in the Cosmos.* Cambridge: Cambridge University Press, 1981.

———. *Human Vices and Human Worth in Dante's "Comedy."* Cambridge: Cambridge University Press, 2000.

———. *Perception and Passion in Dante's "Comedy."* Cambridge: Cambridge University Press, 1993.

Brandeis, Irma. *The Ladder of Vision: A Study of Dante's "Comedy."* Garden City, N.Y.: Anchor Books, 1962.

Brundage, James A. *Law, Sex, and Christian Society in Medieval Europe.* Chicago: University of Chicago Press, 1987.

Cassell, Anthony K. *Dante's Fearful Art of Justice.* Toronto: University of Toronto Press, 1984.

Caesar, Michael, ed. *Dante, the Critical Heritage 1314 (?)–1870.* London: Routledge, 1989.

Cambon, Glauco. *Dante's Craft: Studies in Language and Style.* Minneapolis: University of Minnesota Press, 1969.

Charity, A. C. *Events and Their Afterlife: The Dialectics of Christian Typology in the Bible and Dante.* London: Cambridge University Press, 1966.

Chiavacci Leonardi, Anna M. *La guerra de la pietate: Saggio per una interpretazione dell' "Inferno" di Dante.* Naples: Liguori, 1979.

Cogan, Marc. *The Design in the Wax: The Structure of the "Divine Comedy" and Its Meaning.* Notre Dame, Ind.: University of Notre Dame Press, 1999.

Colish, Marcia L. *Medieval Foundations of the Western Intellectual Tradition 400–1400.* New Haven: Yale University Press, 1997.

Comparetti, Domenico. *Vergil in the Middle Ages.* Translated by E. F. M. Benecke. 1908. Reprint, Hamden, Conn.: Archon Books, 1966.

Contini, Gianfranco. *Un' idea di Dante: Saggi danteschi.* Turin: Einaudi, 1976.

Corti, Maria. *Scritti su Cavalcanti e Dante.* Turin: Einaudi, 2003.

Croce, Benedetto. *La poesia di Dante.* 2d ed. Bari: Laterza, 1921.

Curtius, Ernst Robert. *European Literature and the Latin Middle Ages.* Translated by Willard R. Trask. 1953. Reprint, New York: Harper & Row, 1963.

Davis, Charles T. *Dante's Italy and Other Essays.* Philadelphia: University of Pennsylvania Press, 1984.

De Rougemont, Denis. *Love in the Western World.* Translated by Montgomery Belgion. New York: Harcourt, Brace, 1940. Revised and expanded, with a new postscript, Princeton: Princeton University Press, 1983.

De Sanctis, Francesco. *Lezioni sulla "Divina Commedia."* 1854. Reprint, Bari: Laterza, 1955.

Dronke, Peter. *Dante and Medieval Latin Traditions.* Cambridge: Cambridge University Press, 1986.

Durling, Robert M., and Ronald L. Martinez, eds. *Inferno.* Vol. 1 of *The "Divine Comedy" of Dante Alighieri.* New York: Oxford University Press, 1996.

Eco, Umberto. *Art and Beauty in the Middle Ages.* Translated by Hugh Bredin. New Haven: Yale University Press, 1986.

Ferrante, Joan M. *The Political Vision of the "Divine Comedy."* Princeton: Princeton University Press, 1984.

———. *Woman as Image in Medieval Literature from the Twelfth Century to Dante.* New York: Columbia University Press, 1975. Reprint, Durham, N.C.: Labyrinth Press, 1985.

Ferrucci, Franco. *Il poema del desiderio: Poetica e passione in Dante.* Milan: Leonardo, 1990.

Foster, Kenlem. *The Two Dantes and Other Studies.* Berkeley: University of California Press, 1977.

Fowlie, Wallace. *A Reading of Dante's "Inferno."* Chicago: University of Chicago Press, 1981.

Franke, William. *Dante's Interpretive Journey.* Chicago: University of Chicago Press, 1996.

Freccero, John. *Dante: The Poetics of Conversion.* Edited by Rachel Jacoff. Cambridge: Harvard University Press, 1986.

———, ed. *Dante: A Collection of Critical Essays.* Englewood Cliffs, N.J.: Prentice-Hall, 1965.

Fubini, Mario. *Il peccato di Ulisse e altri scritti danteschi.* Milan: Ricciardi, 1966.

Gilson, Etienne. *Dante and Philosophy.* Translated by David Moore. 1949. Reprint, New York: Harper & Row, 1963.

———. *History of Christian Philosophy in the Middle Ages.* New York: Random House, 1955.

Gilson, Simon A. *Dante and Renaissance Florence.* Cambridge: Cambridge University Press, 2005.

Havely, Nick. *Dante and the Franciscans: Poverty and the Papacy in the "Commedia."* Cambridge: Cambridge University Press, 2004.

Hawkins, Peter S. *Dante's Testaments: Essays in Scriptural Imagination.* Stanford: Stanford University Press, 1999.

Hawkins, Peter S., and Rachel Jacoff, ed. *The Poets' Dante: Twentieth-Century Responses.* New York: Farrar, Strauss and Giroux, 2001.

Hollander, Robert. *Allegory in Dante's "Commedia."* Princeton: Princeton University Press, 1969.

Holmes, George. *Florence, Rome, and the Origins of the Renaissance.* Oxford: Clarendon Press, 1986.

Iannucci, Amilcare A. *Forma ed evento nella "Divina Commedia."* Rome: Bulzoni, 1984.

———. *Dante e la "bella scola" della poesia: Autorità e sfida poetica.* Ravenna: Longo, 1993.

———, ed. *Dante: Contemporary Perspectives.* Toronto: University of Toronto Press, 1997.

Jacoff, Rachel, ed. *Cambridge Companion to Dante.* Cambridge: Cambridge University Press, 1993.

Kantorowicz, Ernst H. *The King's Two Bodies: A Study in Medieval Political Theology.* Princeton: Princeton University Press, 1957.

Kay, Richard. *Dante's Swift and Strong: Essays on "Inferno" XV*. Lawrence: Regents Press of Kansas, 1978.

Kirkpatrick, Robin. *Dante's "Inferno": Difficult and Dead Poetry*. Cambridge: Cambridge University Press, 1987.

Kleiner, John. *Mismapping the Underworld: Daring and Error in Dante's "Comedy."* Stanford: Stanford University Press, 1994.

Lansing, Richard H. *From Image to Idea: A Study of the Simile in Dante's "Commedia."* Ravenna: Longo, 1977.

Lewis, C. S. *The Discarded Image: An Introduction to Medieval and Renaissance Literature*. Cambridge: Cambridge University Press, 1964.

Lindberg, David C. *The Beginnings of Western Science: The European Scientific Tradition in Philosophical, Religious, and Institutional Context, 600 B.C. to A.D. 1450*. Chicago: University of Chicago Press, 1992.

Mandelbaum, Allen, Anthony Oldcorn, and Charles Ross, eds. *Lectura Dantis: Inferno*. Berkeley: University of California Press, 1998.

Mazzeo, Joseph A. *Medieval Cultural Tradition in Dante's "Commedia."* Ithaca, N.Y.: Cornell University Press, 1960. Reprint, New York: Greenwood Press, 1968.

Mazzoni, Francesco, ed. *La Divina Commedia. Inferno*. Florence: Sansoni, 1972.

Mazzotta, Giuseppe. *Dante, Poet of the Desert: History and Allegory in the "Divine Comedy."* Princeton: Princeton University Press, 1979.

———. *Dante's Vision and the Circle of Knowledge*. Princeton: Princeton University Press, 1993.

———, ed. *Critical Essays on Dante*. Boston: G. K. Hall, 1991.

McDougal, Stuart Y, ed. *Dante among the Moderns*. Chapel Hill, N.C.: University of North Carolina Press, 1985.

Menocal, María Rosa. *The Arabic Role in Medieval Literary History: A Forgotten Heritage*. Philadelphia: University of Pennsylvania Press, 1987.

Mercuri, Roberto. *Semantica di Gerione: Il motivo del viaggio nella "Commedia" di Dante*. Rome: Bulzoni, 1984.

Minnis, A. J. *Medieval Theory of Authorship*. 2d ed. Philadelphia: University of Pennsylvania Press, 1988.

Morgan, Alison. *Dante and the Medieval Other World*. Cambridge: Cambridge University Press, 1990.

Murphy, James J. *Rhetoric in the Middle Ages: A History of Rhetorical Theory from Saint Augustine to the Renaissance*. Berkeley: University of California Press, 1974.

Musa, Mark. *Advent at the Gates: Dante's "Comedy."* Bloomington: Indiana University Press, 1974.

————, ed. *Dante's "Inferno": The Indiana Critical Edition*. Bloomington: Indiana University Press, 1995.

Nardi, Bruno. *Dante e la cultura medievale: Nuovi saggi di filosofia dantesca*. 2d ed. Bari: Laterza, 1949.

Noakes, Susan. *Timely Reading: Between Exegesis and Interpretation*. Ithaca, N.Y.: Cornell University Press, 1988.

Padoan, Giorgio. *Il pio Enea, l'empio Ulisse: Tradizione classica e intendimento medievale in Dante*. Ravenna: Longo, 1977.

Pagliaro, Antonino. *Ulisse: Ricerche semantiche sulla "Divina Commedia."* 2 vols. Messina: G. D'Anna, 1967.

Parker, Deborah. *Commentary and Ideology: Dante in the Renaissance*. Durham, N.C.: Duke University Press, 1993.

Pelikan, Jaroslav. *The Growth of Medieval Theology (600–1300)*. Vol. 3 of *The Christian Tradition: A History of the Development of Doctrine*. Chicago: University of Chicago Press, 1978.

Quinones, Ricardo J. *Foundation Sacrifice in Dante's "Commedia."* University Park: Pennsylvania State University Press, 1994.

Raffa, Guy P. *Divine Dialectic: Dante's Incarnational Poetry*. Toronto: University of Toronto Press, 2000.

Reade, W. H. V. *The Moral System of Dante's "Inferno."* 1909. Port Washington, N.Y.: Kennicat Press, 1969.

Sanguinetti, Edoardo. *Interpretazione di Malebolge*. Florence: Olschki, 1961.

Sayers, Dorothy L. *Further Papers on Dante*. London: Methuen, 1957.

————. *Introductory Papers on Dante*. London: Melthuen, 1954. Reprint, New York: Harper, 1955.

Scott, John A. *Understanding Dante*. Notre Dame, Ind.: University of Notre Dame Press, 2004.

Singleton, Charles S. *"Commedia": Elements of Structure*. Vol. 1 of *Dante Studies*. Cambridge: Harvard University Press, 1954.

————, ed. *Inferno: Commentary*. Vol. 1, bk. 2 of *The Divine Comedy*. 3 vols. Princeton: Princeton University Press, 1970–75.

Smalley, Beryl. *The Study of the Bible in the Middle Ages*. 2d ed. Oxford: Blackwell, 1952. Reprint, Notre Dame, Ind.: University of Notre Dame Press, 1964.

Tambling, Jeremy. *Dante and Difference: Writing in the "Commedia."* Cambridge: Cambridge University Press, 1988.

Thompson, David. *Dante's Epic Journeys*. Baltimore: Johns Hopkins University Press, 1974.

Williams, Charles. *The Figure of Beatrice: A Study in Dante*. London: Faber & Faber, 1943. Reprint, New York: Noonday Press, 1961.

INDEX